OVERVIEW

Overview

In order to be successful, companies need to listen and respond to customers' needs and expectations. This helps companies to find out what customers really want from them and what they really think of their services. It also helps them to keep existing customers and attract new ones.

There are five main ways of getting feedback from customers. You can simply observe your customers' behavior, hold a focus group, or conduct a survey. You can also use your salespeople and customer service teams to glean feedback from customers. The Web, e-mail, and social networking allow you to gather feedback from customers in any location. Each provide their own types of data, and companies should choose which ones suit them best.

There are four main steps involved in exploring customer needs. First you need to gather information about the customers' current situation. You then try to discover their desired situation. You also need to investigate any past experiences they may have had with products similar to yours and finally you carry out a gap analysis.

Companies need to manage customer expectations in order to try and provide the final outcome they expect. Customers expect a collaborative relationship, choice, and good value. They also expect prompt response and dispute resolution, a feeling of importance, transparency, two-way communication, and relevant marketing campaigns.

CRM systems help you to efficiently manage your customers' expectations. There are different strategies for this that ensure that the needs of your customers are met quickly and completely. CRM also helps you to provide effective, efficient processes and put your customer at the center of the organization. Finally CRM provides end-to-end connectivity that links the organization with its internal and external customers and its suppliers.

Every organization that wants to move to being more customer focused should have a strategy in place. This customer-focused strategy is built around three key decisions.

The appropriate scale and scope of your strategy is the first crucial decision. This refers to the elements that need to be involved in your organization's customer focus solution.

Next, you must decide the level of integration between these elements. Finally, you need to make the decision whether to create a low, moderate, or high level of customer focus.

When designing your strategy, taken into account the relevant operational strategies for becoming more customer focused that already exist, including Six Sigma and customer relationship management (CRM).

Implementing customer-focus strategies requires a top-down approach involving managers, employees, and customers. The right amount of planning, consideration, and focus is required. The role of management should be clearly defined.

Like in any change-management process, there are several key steps. These include making sure the change is complete and far reaching; generating a sense of urgency and involving the key players; and ensuring managers inspire and motivate their team members, and deal with any conflict that arises.

Another important factor in the change to customer focus is deciding who will be on your implementation team. You must then assign a specific task to each team member, and that member will have the ultimate responsibility for that task.

There are three vital stages to implementing a customer-focused strategy: promoting the strategy; education and training; and improving processes.

There are several advantages to sustaining customer focus in terms of revenue, new customers, and bringing out the best in your employees.

However, there are obstacles that can inhibit sustaining customer focus. These include a lack of management buy-in and no defined strategy. Other difficulties include service quality not being integrated into the company and not listening to customers. Failure to blend customer focus into the training and development process can also cause issues.

Sorin Dumitrascu

Sustaining customer focus revolves around four key elements. There must be management support for the initiative. Creating a system of recognition and rewards that is centered on customer focus is also advised. Also ensure that customer focus is a constant element in any training and development process. Finally, make sure to constantly review progress.

Businesses are using social media to support customer-focused service.

Customers feel they're being heard and this deepens the business-customer relationship. Customers often find they can get their issues resolved quicker and on their terms, as opposed to dealing with traditional help desks and waiting for customer service representatives to return their calls.

Companies are generating important competitive insights through social media. They are then using this information to provide more unique and tailored experiences for their customers. They can also learn more about their competitors strengths and weaknesses and adjust their strategies accordingly.

But the investment can be high. Having ways to measure social media's ROI provides necessary proof for further investment. Tracking data like customer retention ratio, number of issues identified and responded to, and process innovations can help compare costs to benefits. Also, monitoring the amount of content users contribute, sales, and the number of fans can give you projected revenues.

Knowledge management is used in customer interaction for a number of purposes. It can increase innovation and help companies quickly release new products and services. As well, KM helps solve customer problems by rapidly making knowledge available.

KM, when integrated with CRM, helps make more information available to those accessing customer service. And an adaptive KM system changes and grows with each new interaction and raises your business's information-gathering abilities to the next level.

Then, once KM systems are functional in your customer service environment, you'll recognize the benefits. Your business will be more efficient and consistent in customer service interactions. You'll also be able to retain existing customers and win new ones due to positive customer interactions and satisfied customers. Finally, you'll be able to improve processes through having valuable information available to those executing the processes.

Once your business begins to understand how mobile technology is applied in customer service, you'll begin to recognize the advantages. Knowing how to provide content more easily to customers, understanding how to give them 24/7 access, and recognizing how the technology can be used to build customer rapport will benefit your business and get mobile technology working for you.

Then you can consider some key concepts associated with mobile CRM to help make your decision to move forward a reality. The positives include the fact that mobile users can help build CRM databases. Also when customers opt-in, there's an opportunity for deeper CRM penetration. This is linked to the personal nature of mobile technology and increases CRM system value.

Sorin Dumitrascu

Other considerations when deciding to implement mobile CRM are that rapid change brings instability along with innovation, so you should examine your business's core strategy before exploiting the potential of mobile CRM. Considering these concepts will ensure your investment and software choices pay off.

CHAPTER ONE

Identifying and Managing Customer Expectations

Why listen to customers?

Can you remember the last time you felt listened to as a customer? Did it make a difference in your experience? More importantly, can you remember the last time you felt you were not listened to? Customers expect their needs and expectations to be met. What separates companies with great customer service from the rest is the degree to which they listen to their customers. Customer-centric organizations attempt to meet customer needs and expectations by listening to the feedback they receive.

To stay competitive in the global marketplace, companies must encourage feedback from customers. And they must listen to this feedback in order to understand what their customers want.

However, it's not enough to just listen. Companies must also act on what customers tell them. This shows customers that they were listened to and that their feedback is valued.

Customer Focus

Companies also need to be proactive in getting feedback. The most obvious way to do this is to have a formal feedback and complaints process. This encourages customers to communicate with the company.

A month ago, Mike complained to one of his suppliers that deliveries were arriving late on almost every occasion. The customer service representative reassured him that the company was sorry about this and that it wouldn't happen again. Mike explained that he couldn't have this happening because it negatively impacts his service to his own customers.

The next two deliveries were still late. The delays were having a serious impact on Mike's business, so he decided to change suppliers. Mike explained that it negatively impacts service to his own customers.

Mike's experience with his initial supplier is an example of the customer not being listened to. The fact that Mike made a complaint that was then subsequently ignored made the experience worse than if no complaint had been made at all.

This negative interaction could have been turned into a positive one. All the supplier had to do was listen to the complaint and act on it so that future deliveries weren't late. Remember, customer service involves listening and acting.

Mike decided to move his business to a new supplier. This supplier listened to what Mike really wanted and guaranteed that he would always get his deliveries on time. This means that Mike is a happy customer and is more likely to recommend the supplier's services to others.

Question

What are the benefits of listening to customers?

Options:
1. You find out what your customers really want
2. You find out what customers really think about your services
3. You retain existing customers and attract new customers
4. You can give the impression of caring without having to make any real changes
5. When you make the effort to listen, your customers will buy more products and services 6. You know what prices to charge for your products

Answer:
Option 1: This option is correct. The only way to give customers what they want is to first understand what that is through listening.

Option 2: This option is correct. Sometimes listening involves getting negative feedback through complaints. It's important to know what your customers really think of your products or services so that you can adjust them when necessary.

Option 3: This option is correct. By listening and acting on what you learn, you make customers feel valued and satisfied. They're more likely to reward your efforts with loyalty and recommend you to others, which attracts more business.

Option 4: This option is incorrect. Listening to customers is only successful when you act on what you're told. Customers feel irritated if they give feedback that's subsequently ignored.

Option 5: This option is incorrect. While it's true that customer needs should guide the product and service choices you make, listening to your customers won't necessarily lead to them to buy more products and services from your business

Option 6: This option is incorrect. Pricing can be a key competitive strategy, but customers shouldn't dictate prices. A company may compete on quality or speed, for instance, and therefore meet its customer needs in different ways.

Ways of getting feedback

Given the global nature of modern business, listening to customers is more important than ever. There are a number of ways companies can gather information about customer needs and expectations and companies must carefully consider the most appropriate methods. Each one is suitable for different situations, and sometimes a combination of two or more works best.

Five useful ways to gather feedback from your customers are through observation, focus groups, surveys, salespeople and customer service, and the Web, e-mail, and social networking.

One of the simplest and most cost-effective methods of gathering information is simply observing your customers as they shop for your product or use your service.

Note how they search for, purchase, and use your product or service. With their permission, you might even walk around with customers, asking them about the decisions they're making along the way.

Customer Focus

One way to do this is to go through the customer experience yourself.

The brand manager of a hair care company is observing how customers shop for hair care items. He's particularly interested in whether there's a large majority that always go for the same brands, or if more customers spend time looking at different products before they decide. After taking some notes, he then politely asks a few customers how they came to their decisions. This information is then reported to the brand's product manager.

Another option is to use a more hands-on method for getting feedback by holding a focus group. Focus groups are used when richer, more detailed data is required. A representative sample of customers, or potential customers, gathers to discuss certain elements of a product or service, guided by a moderator.

Focus groups are a qualitative method of getting feedback. Although the facilitator will have a plan for key items to be discussed, a free flow of ideas and opinions is encouraged. Focus groups are best when you require a more dynamic method of gathering information. They can elicit detailed insights into customer needs and attitudes.

Electronic focus groups can be even more effective than face-to-face ones. They often result in franker responses, each participant having an equal opportunity to comment, and more suggestions for improvements. There are no geographic restrictions with online focus groups so their reach is great and can be used to access larger sample sizes.

A mobile phone company is holding a focus group with ten people to discuss various elements of their preferences for and uses of mobile phones.

This focus group shows the mobile phone company that it has three distinct customer segments. The first segment likes up-to-date mobile devices with all the features. The second segment represents teenagers and young adults who want a phone with a good camera, but not necessarily all the extras. And the third segment wants a basic, sturdy, and inexpensive phone that can be easily replaced.

The focus group also provides the company with two interesting suggestions for improvements and new services. Now the company is considering offering appropriate insurance policies for each category of phone it sells. The company is also introducing customer service training for all sales staff members so that they can explain phone features clearly to customers, without using technical jargon.

Question

Which statements about focus groups are true?

Options:

1. Focus groups can provide richer, more detailed data than other feedback methods.

2. Although a moderator guides the conversation and influences the issues discussed, a free flow of ideas and opinions is encouraged.

3. Focus groups are a good way of gathering large-scale feedback from a large number of customers.

4. Focus groups observe customer behavior with a product or service.

Answer:

Customer Focus

Option 1: This option is correct. The nature of focus groups allows participants to give feedback in their own words. This allows for much more detailed responses and the opportunity for more accurate interpretation of customer needs.

Option 2: This option is correct. A moderator facilitates the conversation to keep things on track and make sure that certain issues and questions are discussed. Within this context, participants are encouraged to chat freely about their opinions and attitudes.

Option 3: This option is incorrect. Focus groups use small samples, as it would be difficult to hold a real-time conversation with a large group of customers at the same time.

Option 4: This option is incorrect. Focus groups elicit direct responses from customers about their thoughts and use of a product. It's not an observational method.

Surveys offer another option and are a tried and tested way of getting feedback from customers. They're used when a company requires quantitative information about what it's doing well and where it has problems. They can also tell you which category of your customer base is having what type of experience.

A survey is used to reveal who your customers are and what they think of you. You should use a survey if you want information on reasons customers wouldn't return to your product or store, or reasons they didn't buy your product and chose another instead.

Getting the right results from your surveys comes down to designing the questions carefully. This enables you to capture information that you can turn into meaningful changes and improvements.

You can choose from a variety of surveys, including online surveys and mail surveys. However, there are some guidelines that apply to all types of surveys. You need to set survey objectives and keep within the optimum survey length. Also, use closed-ended and open-ended questions, and ensure an adequate response rate. Finally, tell customers about your findings.

See each guideline to learn more about it.

Set survey objectives

To set survey objectives, you need to ask yourself whether you want to find out about satisfaction levels or how customers prefer to use your products. Different companies have different objectives, and some will have more than one.

Keep within optimum survey length

The optimum survey length is usually about ten minutes. When designing your survey, it's important to pay attention to length. If it's too long, respondents tend to lose interest or answer haphazardly.

Use closed-ended or open-ended questions

Closed-ended question responses are easier to analyze on a mass scale. However, open-ended question responses, given in the customers' own words, can be very informative when it comes to assessing attitudes and receiving suggestions for improvement.

Ensure adequate response

It's critical to ensure an adequate survey response to make your results truly representative and prevent wasted costs. Incentivize people to respond to your survey by offering prize draws or coupons, or simply by promoting it well.

Tell customers about your findings

Customer Focus

You must reassure customers that you've taken notice of what they said. If they took the time to fill out a survey, it's only right that you give them feedback on the changes you're making as a result of their responses.

A company contacts customers after any sale or interaction and asks them to fill out an online survey about their experience. The company then gathers the results, analyzes them, and provides this information to company employees to alert them to any customer service or product issues. Information on changes that are being made as a result of the surveys is then provided to customers via the company's web site. This helps to retain customers and attract new ones.

Sometimes a simple option is best. Salespeople and customer service teams are another way to get feedback and are one of the best sources a company has. The reason for this is that customer service employees deal with prospective and existing customers on a daily basis.

Frontline employees are best placed to talk to customers face-to-face about how they feel regarding your product or service. Queries can be dropped into conversation in a natural and noninvasive way. The employees can then feed the responses back to their managers.

For example, you can build a feedback mechanism into the process at the point of sale. Frontline staff members are in a key position here to get information from customers in each and every interaction. Looking after your customer service and sales teams pays off. Many customers report higher levels of satisfaction when these staff members report similar levels of satisfaction. This makes sense, as these employees act as the face of the company and typically have the greatest amount of interaction with customers.

The final method for gathering feedback is through the Web, e-mail, and social networking. These methods are all standard practices of communication for modern, customer-centric companies.

The Internet provides almost limitless opportunities to reach out and communicate with customers. It can be through a company's web site, personalized e-mails, or a company's social networking presence.

Customer measures can be calculated via online interactions. For instance, you can find out how many people are visiting your site through traffic statistics. You can also determine conversion rates, which tell you how many of those visits were converted into sales.

Customer service on the Internet also covers social networking sites. Companies that can maintain an engaging online presence over these platforms are often able to connect with their customers in unique ways. For example, companies can garner valuable feedback by hosting special chat sessions, competitions featuring give-aways and prizes, and other personalized and unique opinion polling techniques through these platforms.

Question

Which statements describing some of the feedback methods are true?

Options:

1. Salespeople and customer service employees are one of the most cost-effective feedback sources you can use

2. Salespeople and frontline staff can gather feedback from customers easily feedback at the point of sale

Customer Focus

3. Web, e-mail, and social networking enable companies to interact with customers on a more personal level

4. Salespeople and customer service employees are a good source of quantitative feedback

5. Web, e-mail, and social networking involve a simple formula that any company can follow

6. Salespeople and customer service teams will automatically provide feedback without having a specifically designed process in place

Answer:

Option 1: This option is correct. Salespeople and customer service employees can gather feedback in a natural and noninvasive way through their daily interactions.

Option 2: This option is correct. Frontline staff can consistently gather feedback at the point of sale. Option 3: This option is correct. Web, e-mail, and social networking cross boundaries through the

almost limitless opportunities of the Internet, but can still be made personal.

Option 4: This option is incorrect. If you require quantitative, general feedback, a survey is the best method to use.

Option 5: This option is incorrect. Using the Web, e-mail, or social networking doesn't have to be complicated. However, companies need to design their own individual ways to use these tools.

Option 6: This option is incorrect. It's important to have a suitably designed process in place to encourage all employees to do this consistently.

Many customers are happy to provide feedback but it's important that it's done in an appropriate way. Feedback methods can be flawed in a number of ways. If your methods are flawed, customers can become irritated and may be driven away.

One of the most common mistakes that companies make is not responding to feedback. When customers have been asked for their opinions, they're likely to look out for changes to be implemented as a result. When this doesn't happen, they may feel that their time has been wasted.

Avoid inconveniencing customers when asking for feedback. Feedback-gathering methods should be designed so they are engaging, easy to use and completely hassle-free.

Another mistake is not leaving space for feedback on a questionnaire or survey. Customers may feel short-changed if they take the time to answer the questions that the company asks but aren't given the opportunity to add their own opinions also.

Another potential flaw is not giving respondents enough time to think about their feedback. Some feedback methods such as face-to-face or phone questionnaires might get inaccurate answers because they force customers to come up with their answers on the spot.

Requesting feedback that's irrelevant to the customer is another mistake. This could alienate your customers because they may feel that you're not really interested in their concerns.

Question

Match each company's scenario to the appropriate feedback technique it requires.

Customer Focus

Options:

A. A software supplier wants detailed feedback about how customers use applications over time

B. A hair salon wants to ensure it captures customer information at the point of sale

C. A global cosmetics company wants to engage with customers across the world

D. A government agency wants general feedback from customers about its service

E. A store manager is curious to know how customers browse for products

Targets:

1. Focus groups
2. Salespeople and customer service
3. Web, e-mail, and social networking
4. Surveys
5. Observing your customers

Answer:

A computer company looking for specific feedback would choose a focus group.

A company looking to get consistent feedback would use a process that involves salespeople and customer service teams.

A company can use its "voice" to engage with customers across the world through the Web, e-mail, and social networking.

The best way to get general feedback and data from a large group of customers is to use surveys. You can get general feedback on how customers browse by observing customers as they shop.

Why explore customer needs?

Modern companies are thinking from the outside in. Customers often have ideas about what they should or shouldn't buy. For example, most people know they should buy healthy food. However, these ideas don't always align with their actual buying habits. Some customers might spend more money on fast food than on healthy food. In order to maintain a competitive edge, companies must have a clear picture of what their customers really want and actually buy.

But customers often can't effectively articulate their needs. They may know what they want, but they can't clearly explain it. This can make it difficult for you to determine what products or services to offer them.

In order to understand their needs, you have to build a holistic picture of your customers. This can help you decide which products and services to target at which customers.

Customer Focus

Even if customers are able to articulate what they mean, it's important that the company digs deeper to understand exactly how they feel about key aspects of your business and why. For example, basic terms such as "service" and "quality" may mean different things to different customers.

Exploring customer needs relies on asking the right questions. There are general guidelines when asking appropriate exploration questions. You should start with broad questions and then get specific. Try to build on previous responses and remember that it helps to keep questions simple. Also, you should focus on your customer's desired benefits and try to maintain a consultative attitude by emphasizing that you're interested in the best outcome for your customer.

When exploring your customers' needs, it helps to carry out four basic steps. The first involves investigating customers' current situation and then identifying their desired situation. After these two steps, try to close the gap by investigating their relevant past experiences with existing products and finally by carrying out a customer gap analysis.

Current and desired situation

The first step of the process is finding out your customers' current situation. Talk to them and show them that you have a genuine interest in what's important to them. Try to determine their needs and how you can satisfy those needs. Show them that you want to help them get to where they want to be.

Try to discover customers' urgency in buying a new product or service. Ask about their criteria for buying. This means investigating customers' psychological constraints – the requirements they have for making purchasing decisions. It could be that they're looking for the best price or the best quality, for instance.

Exploring current circumstances also includes trying to discover if customers have money constraints. This can affect the pricing of your offering.

Political influences, and whether or not they're the key decision makers, also count as important information.

Customer Focus

You may have noted that you could explore your customers' needs by asking them appropriate questions about their situation and buying constraints. Consider this example of investigating one customer's current situation. A car salesperson meets with a potential customer and suggests they sit down to discuss what she's looking for.

Follow along as the salesperson, Martin, investigates the current situation of the customer, Sheila.

Martin: Hi there, I'm Martin, welcome to our showroom. What kind of car do you drive at the moment?

Sheila: I'm driving a small compact but I had a baby last month and we want something bigger and safer for our family car.

Martin: So this would be your second car?

Sheila: Yes, my husband has his own car but we want something practical and suitable for the whole family. Our main priorities are safety and reliability. My last car let me down so many times...

Martin: What kind of price range did you have in mind?

Sheila: If I find something that I think is suitable for us, I'll return another day to discuss the financial options.

By having an initial conversation with the customer, the sales executive is able to explore her current situation. He discovers that she has recently had a baby. Her priorities are safety and reliability for her new family. The salesperson needs to ensure that he finds a solution that aligns with the customer's current situation taking all her constraints into account.

Question

What factors should you try to find out about when exploring a customer's current situation?

Options:
1. Psychological constraints
2. Buying criteria
3. Who the key decision maker is
4. Urgency in buying
5. How long it will take the customer to make a decision before buying
6. What the customer knows about your company and products

Answer:

Option 1: This option is correct. There are a number of psychological factors that affect a customer's priorities. You should explore these and focus on them when trying to bridge the customer's needs gap.

Option 2: This option is correct. When exploring the customer's current situation, you should try to discover the person's decision-making characteristics.

Option 3: This option is correct. You should discreetly try to discover whether or not you are dealing with the key decision maker when you are discussing a customer's current situation.

Option 4: This option is correct. Knowing how fast a customer needs to make a decision affects the current situation and how you will try to fill the needs gap.

Option 5: This option is incorrect. It's no harm to have this information if it's offered voluntarily. However, your aim is to focus on customer priorities and not your own by exploring the customer's current situation and building trust.

Option 6: This option is incorrect. Exploring the current situation is about discovering what the customer's priorities are. The customer is only interested in how you can help.

Once you have discovered customers' current circumstances, you should explore their desired situation. Explore what they'd like to achieve, focusing on the features and benefits that are important to them.

Exploring customers' desired situations should dictate what services and products you might offer, if any. It's no use offering them a perfect solution for something that just isn't a priority for them.

Try to ask relevant questions about where they would like to be in their business or what they'd like to achieve personally. Talk about what they're not currently happy with and what their goals and aspirations are for the future.

A sales executive in an electronics store is speaking with a customer about music systems. The customer has asked about quality speakers for a CD player. In conversation, the salesperson discovers that he isn't happy with the sound quality from his system and has problems with CD storage. The customer says he'd like it if moving and storing his music was simpler. The salesperson suggests a digital system, which the customer thinks is the perfect solution.

Question

An executive at a media company is meeting with a new potential client to discuss their requirements. The client company states that it only wants to run a once-off promotional advertising campaign for a new product. However, in the conversation, the media executive asks about the company's other products and discovers that it has an interesting selection. The executive also finds out through his questions that the company recently had a setback when one of its products was given negative press coverage. After further discussion, the client admits that this had an effect on its sales and that its struggling to keep prices down as a result.

What information did the media executive glean about the client company's current and desired circumstances?

Options:

1. The client company had an interesting range of products in addition to the one it wanted to promote

2. The client company had suffered a recent setback when it received negative press about one of its products

3. The company was under financial constraints as sales had dropped

4. The company wished to keep prices down and promote its products to improve sales

5. The client company wants only one service from the media company and was not open to buying other services

6. The client company has no money to pay for more services

Answer:

Option 1: This option is correct. The executive explored the current situation of the client and discovered that there were more opportunities for advertising interesting products.

Option 2: This option is correct. Through exploring the client company's current situation, the executive discovered that this recent setback was affecting the company's image.

Option 3: This option is correct. The executive discovered through his exploration that a recent setback was affecting the company's sales and finances as a result.

Option 4: This option is correct. The executive discovered that despite financial constraints it was a priority to the client to keep prices down and sales up.

Option 5: This option is incorrect. The client did appear to want one product initially. However, through exploration of the client company's current and desired situation, the executive discovered that he could offer more than one solution to its needs.

Option 6: This option is incorrect. The executive discovered that the client was under financial constraints but that doesn't necessarily mean that there is no money to pay for necessary services.

Closing the gap

It's often the case that existing or potential customers have had a bad experience in the past with similar products to yours. Before you can close the needs gap, you should try to probe customers about their relevant past experiences.

It may be that they had a problem dealing with your company in the past or that they have used a product similar to yours and it didn't do what they expected. If customers don't mention any relevant experiences, ask about their past experiences. These experiences may be coloring a potential customers' opinions unnecessarily.

So emphasize why your service is different. Even if they have had good experiences with similar products or services, you should explain to customers what differentiates your product.

Customers will usually be happy to tell you why they weren't happy with a similar product. And you'll be better able to address the issues. If there are no issues then you should move on with your analysis.

Consider this example. An account executive from an online management magazine is speaking to a prospective client, the CEO of a large corporation. Follow along as she investigates the client's past experience with existing products.

Karen: We provide an online management magazine to many large corporations such as yours. It's an excellent resource for up-to-date research. Would this be of interest to your company?

Pamela: It does sound interesting. But I'm not sure about online services.

Karen: OK can I ask you what concerns you have about them exactly? Perhaps I can explain how our service is different.

Pamela: I don't like subscribing to services online. I've found from experience that it's very difficult to opt out when you no longer require the service and they often try to lock you into long contracts.

Karen: Our service doesn't operate that way at all. Our customers pay on a month-by-month basis. We don't ask customers to commit to contracts. We call each month to check that everything is OK and most customers renew each time as they find it so useful. I guarantee that you can opt out whenever you wish.

Pamela: OK that sounds fair. I'll take the one month trial then please.

In the previous example, Karen probed the potential client about her past experience with an existing product. By asking Pamela what exactly she was apprehensive about, Karen was able to address her concerns. This experience was coloring Pamela's attitude toward online magazines but Karen reassured her by emphasizing how her service was different.

Question

Which statements apply to investigating relevant past experiences with customers?

Options:

1. If customers don't mention past experiences, you should probe them during your conversation about their relevant experiences with similar products

2. You should try to emphasize how your product is different when necessary

3. If customers say that they haven't had any relevant experiences you should keep probing as they may be reluctant to share this information

4. You should remember that the only relevant experiences relating to similar products are the bad ones

Answer:

Option 1: This option is correct. Customers may not mention a relevant experience so you should try to discover if they've had any as it could be affecting their judgement.

Option 2: This option is correct. A customer may have had a bad past experience with a product similar to yours. You need to address this because it may be coloring their decision making.

Option 3: This option is incorrect. If customers say they've no relevant past experiences with similar products then move on with your gap analysis.

Option 4: This option is incorrect. It's possible that customers have had relevant experiences with products similar to yours that weren't bad. You should still try to discover them and differentiate your offering.

Once you have explored the customer's current and desired situation and any relevant past experiences, you have the information you need to carry out a gap analysis. Gap analyses look at deficiencies that exist in the market and how to fill them. Try to start broad with your analysis by looking at supply and demand gaps, then address how you can help each individual customer specifically.

When carrying out a gap analysis for one customer or for a group of customers, you should try to examine supply and demand gaps. Select each of the gaps to learn more about it.

Supply gaps

Supply gaps exist where companies offer services or products that customers can get elsewhere at lower prices or more conveniently. The best example are services that were traditionally provided by agents but are now offered online without the middle man.

Demand gaps

A demand gap exists when customers are willing to pay for better service or product offerings that aren't currently available. You can try to find out from your exploration of customers' current and desired situations what offerings customers would be willing to pay for if you enhanced your own range.

If you have a product or service that suits what customers are looking for, emphasize how it helps their particular situation.

If you don't, then try to build a long-term relationship of trust so that they may shop with you in the future.

When carrying out a gap analysis with your customers, examine the information you've gathered in your exploration. Investigate whether there are demand gaps that you can move in to fill. If there are supply gaps, investigate what ways you can enhance your offering to increase its value to customers.

There are things that can go wrong in a gap analysis. For example, don't try to make, or force, your products or services to fit where they don't as a solution to a problem.

And avoid focusing on your own priorities rather than those of the customer.

When trying to fill a gap in the market with an enhanced offering, investigate to ensure it's something that customers will actually be willing to pay for, and that it's something you can afford.

Consider this example of closing the gap. A woman's wear boutique finds that it's having to compete with lower cost online retailers. The owner examines her customer base's current and desired situation and discovers that choice and convenience are priorities. She also discovers that customers like to buy one-off items. To fill this supply gap, the owner enhances her offering by introducing online shopping and holding exclusive online sales for members only.

Case Study: Question 1 of 3
Scenario:

For your convenience, the case study is repeated with each question.

Kevin works for a property development company and he is about to carry out a gap analysis. Select the learning aid Carrying Out a Gap Analysis at a Construction Company to learn about his experience.

Customer Focus

Help Kevin set achievable goals by answering the questions in order.

Question:

What information did Harry glean about Kevin's situation?

Options:

1. Kevin has financial constraints due to the fact that he is stretched across a number of projects at the moment

2. Kevin had a bad past experience with a similar service when he used one of Harry's competitors

3. Kevin wants the job finished as quickly as possible and wants to keep the materials and finishings to a high standard

4. He made sure that Kevin was aware of all the relevant facts about his company and their achievements

5. That Kevin was in a rush to finish and therefore would pay a high price for the work

Answer:

Option 1: This option is correct. By exploring Kevin's current situation, Harry discovered that he's under pressure with a lot of projects running at the moment.

Option 2: This option is correct. Harry discovered through his exploration that Kevin had a relevant bad experience with a similar service. Harry needs to address this.

Option 3: This option is correct. Harry discovered through his exploration that Kevin's priorities for his desired situation are to finish the job quickly and to maintain his reputation for high standards.

Option 4: This option is incorrect. This information was not needed for Harry to carry out a gap analysis.

Option 5: This option is incorrect. Kevin had three priorities, one of them was to finish quickly. However, the other two were to finish to a high standard and to keep costs down.

Case Study: Question 2 of 3

What did Harry's gap analysis establish about the services he should offer to Kevin in this scenario?

Options:

1. Harry should offer to finish the project quickly but to a high standard
2. Harry should stress his company's reliability and care in maintaining a high standard
3. There are no other companies that can offer Kevin what he's looking for
4. Harry should focus on offering the best finish date before all else

Answer:

Option 1: This option is correct. Two of Kevin's priorities were to finish quickly and to still maintain a high standard.

Option 2: This option is correct. Harry discovered that Kevin had a bad past experience. He therefore needed to address this in his pitch and emphasize how his service is different.

Option 3: This option is incorrect. Harry isn't aware at this stage whether Kevin has met with other companies and whether they can offer what he's looking for.

Option 4: This option is incorrect. Kevin is also concerned with maintaining a high standard so this needs to be part of what Harry offers.

Case Study: Question 3 of 3

What mistake did Harry make in the scenario?

Customer Focus

Options:
1. He spent too long talking
2. He asked too many questions
3. He presented information about his own products first

Answer:

Option 1: This option is incorrect. It's good practice to spend time discussing priorities with your customer and exploring their needs.

Option 2: This option is incorrect. Harry asked the right amount of questions as part of a normal conversation investigating his customer's needs.

Option 3: This is the correct option. Exploring customer needs is about finding out what their priorities are and trying to match them with solutions, not the other way around.

Strategies for managing expectations

Customers are the life blood of any organization. Organizations aim to provide a final outcome that meets customer expectations as closely as possible. Companies need to know what customers want so they can focus their offerings to make the most profit possible. To do this, they need to know which products or customers have the most growth potential. They also need to know which products or services are the most or least profitable and which customers will endorse new offerings.

Customers have expectations that may change over time. Sometimes expectations can be created by the company, and some expectations come from the product itself or even from competitors.

You cannot presume you're aware of what a customer's expectations are. You have to ask.

Question

Rank the customer expectations you think are most important for your customers.

Customer Focus

Options:
A. A collaborative relationship with the organization they're using
B. Choice and good value
C. Prompt response and dispute resolution
D. Personalization and a feeling of importance
E. Transparency and accountability in their interactions with an organization

Answer:
A collaborative relationship with the organization they're using is ranked the most important. Customers expect most of all that the companies they deal with will move with them and always try to know and provide what they really want.

Choice and good value is ranked the second most important. Customers expect good choice and value for money from a company's products and services as their second priority.

Prompt response and dispute resolution is ranked the third most important. Thirdly, customers value organizations that have efficient and effective processes. This makes for a smoother experience each time they interact with the company.

Personalization and a feeling of importance is ranked the fourth most important. The fourth priority for customers is that they're put at the center of the organization. Customers expect to feel important and to receive personalized attention from companies they deal with.

Transparency and accountability in their interactions with an organization is ranked the fifth most important. The fifth priority for customers is that they expect companies to be honest about their processes and to be accountable in their customer services.

Customers have come to expect many things from organizations. They want to have a collaborative relationship with the organizations they use. They want choice and good value, prompt response and dispute resolution, plus personalization and a feeling of importance. They also expect firms to practice transparency and accountability in their processes. And they expect firms to maintain a consistent presence and two-way communication, as well as marketing relevancy in targeted campaigns.

There are several strategies you can use to manage customer expectations: know what your customers value

watch competitors

say no if necessary to avoid making promises you can't keep, and keep your promises

You should know what your customers value in your product or service. There may be combinations of values such as speed of service or low-cost suppliers that make your operations more efficient.

However, these values are of no use unless they are what your customers value most.

You need to evaluate your market and customer segments and gear your offerings to serve them and you better.

Consider this example. A restaurant manager wants to offer cheap, fast menu items to improve lunch-time traffic. He keeps staff numbers low, hires an unqualified chef, and buys the cheapest supplies. He offers cheap, fast meals at lunch but customers are unhappy with the quality of the food. They would prefer to pay a bit more for better food that's served quickly. The manager decides to invest in more staff, a qualified chef, and fresher supplies, which increases lunch traffic immensely.

You should watch what your competitors are doing. Competitors may be making promises they can't keep. It's possible to swoop in and "rescue" a customer from a bad experience. However, you should always aim to be better than competitors so that customers come to you in the first place.

Listen to what competitors are promising and inform your customers in a consultative manner what's possible to expect and not to expect. Customers will then notice that you always keep your promises and often exceed them in comparison to competitors.

The restaurant manager noticed that one or two of his competitors in the locality were advertising fast, cheap, and good-quality lunches. He decides to emphasize in its advertisements and customer interactions that the restaurant will offer only home-made, quality food at the best prices possible.

The restaurant manager informs customers that this kind of efficient service and gourmet quality costs a little more. However, he emphasizes that he can guarantee that the food is the best quality possible at reasonable prices.

When thinking of times you found it difficult to manage all your customers' needs, you may have felt afraid to refuse some of their demands.

Remember that managing expectations effectively will occasionally mean saying no. This is acceptable from time to time, and customers will come to respect your integrity in only offering commitments you can stand by.

Providing you attempt to meet expectations in many other ways, saying no to something you can't deliver on can be part of an honest relationship with your customers.

At the restaurant, some customers are asking if they can get meals delivered to local offices. While it's something he may look into in the future, the restaurant manager considers it would jeopardize the efficiency and quality of the service at the restaurant.

The manager feels that the service is best offered in-house where the quality of the food and numbers of staff for efficient service can be guaranteed.

Having gone to the trouble of evaluating customer expectations and offering them what they want, it's critical to keep your promises.

Nothing puts off customers like when they have been assured of a benefit to a service and then don't receive it. When you make promises to customers, they expect you to keep them.

At this critical point in the restaurant's service overhaul, customers have come to expect the guarantees of fast service, quality food, and value-for-money prices. It would be detrimental to business if the restaurant compromises on any of these key promises. The manager makes it a priority to serve good food efficiently and to keep prices reasonable. Customers expect you to keep your promises.

Question

A consumer goods company wants to improve its product range.

Which strategies could it use to manage customer expectations of its products?

Options:

Customer Focus

1. Find out what products customers are really looking for at the moment
2. Analyze competitor companies and the products they are offering
3. Say no to products that are not profitable or that might compromise the company's value promises
4. Ensure to keep its value-promises to customers so that they know what they can expect from the company
5. Try to source and stock every single item customers request
6. Drop the prices on as many products as possible to please customers and attract new ones

Answer:

Option 1: This option is correct. One of the ways to manage customer expectations is to know what they really want.

Option 2: This option is correct. Analyzing what competitors are doing is an effective way of finding out what your own customers expect.

Option 3: This option is correct. Saying no is sometimes the most effective way to manage your customers' expectations.

Option 4: This option is correct. An important part of managing customers' expectations is always keeping your promises.

Option 5: This option is incorrect. It would be unsustainable and unprofitable to stock everything a customer might want. It's more beneficial to manage expectations effectively.

Option 6: This option is incorrect. Lowering prices on many items is not a strategy for managing customer expectations and may even lead to a company being unprofitable.

Customer Relationship Management

Customer Relationship Management, or CRM for short, concerns the relationship between the organization and its customers. CRM refers to the methods companies use to track the behavior of customers and meet their expectations. This type of customer management relies on a company having up-to-date information about all of its customers all the time. In exchange for this information, customers enjoy benefits such as bonus points and loyalty reward systems.

A CRM software system gathers information about a company's customers and analyzes it. An example of this would be store discount cards. When customers pay for goods, their card is scanned. The item details are then entered into the store's database so that the business has an accurate idea of what each consumer buys.

Once this information is analyzed, the store can adjust its marketing campaigns to suit its customers and increase sales. It may even personalize offers sent through the mail according to what a customer buys.

Using the card also brings benefits to the customers. Every time these cards are used, they earn points and save money on their purchases.

CRM software systems enable companies to improve customer service. When customer service representatives are interacting with customers, they can view relevant information about the customers. This enables them to provide a more personalized service. And it makes customers feel they're part of a two-way communication process with the company.

Businesses can also use automated CRM applications to analyze customer complaints or compliments and change business processes accordingly. Technology makes this a relatively simple process but one that has a huge impact on the efficiency of the business according to the customer.

For example, a supermarket chain notices from its customer data that when cheaper alternatives of everyday items are offered, customers usually purchase that product. This led the chain to offer a larger range of cheaper alternatives and market them heavily to increase customer numbers.

Question

Which are characteristics of a CRM system?

Options:

1. It gathers information about a company's customers and analyzes it

2. It collects information that enables companies to tailor their marketing campaigns to suit different customers

3. It allows the service representative to see customers' relevant information when interacting with them

4. It's an efficient way of managing customer services that can replace traditional customer service teams

5. CRM is primarily an IT system that doesn't impact other levels of the business

Answer:

Option 1: This option is correct. Information is gathered in a centralized system and analyzed so that the company can learn more about its customers' habits.

Option 2: This option is correct. The information gathered in a CRM system can be analyzed to help companies tailor their marketing campaigns to their customers.

Option 3: This option is correct. Customers feel they're dealing with an efficient company that knows them as they don't have to repeat information in each interaction.

Option 4: This option is incorrect. CRM systems help the efficiency of customer management but they don't replace the human side of customer service.

Option 5: This option is incorrect. The information held in a CRM system is centralized and makes every level of an organization more efficient in its processes.

CRM can help manage customer expectations in a number of ways. The needs of your customers are met quickly and completely and it provides effective, efficient processes. CRM also provides systems and processes that put the customer at the center of the organization. Finally, it provides end-to-end connectivity that links the organization with internal and external customers and suppliers.

Meeting the needs of customers quickly and completely is a huge benefit of CRM systems. Many CRM software packages have detailed note-taking and contact systems. These enable customer service and sales professionals to record customer interactions.

This way when customers communicate with the company, these representatives can easily access the details of each conversation the customer has had with the company. Having this information prevents repetition in your communications with customers, which is unprofessional.

As CRM provides a centralized system of information, customers don't have to explain their situation each time they contact you. This makes your service more comprehensive, efficient, and professional from their perspective. The fact that you understand and anticipate their expectations encourages customers to use your products and services again and recommend you to others.

A customer of an online bank calls to check the status of an ATM card she ordered. She's asked to enter her account number and security information. When she gets through to a customer service representative, he's able to greet her by name and access her recent conversations with the company. He reviews the data he needs to check her order status. She's relieved that she doesn't have to repeat her details when she speaks to the representative.

Another benefit of CRM systems is that they enable effective and efficient processes. Customer relationships happen on many levels of the organization where the same customer may speak to different personnel in various interactions.

Customer Focus

By using CRM data, companies can design processes that enable them to efficiently deliver customer satisfaction.

CRM allows companies to share relevant data among all relevant parts of the company. The shared data allows informed decisions and follow-ups to be made efficiently at each level, saving the customer and the company valuable time.

In the online bank example, the bank's centralized CRM system allowed the representative to serve the customer efficiently. The customer had spoken with a different representative when she initially called to order the replacement ATM card.

This didn't affect the customer's experience when she calls again, as the representative recorded the initial order on her account in the CRM system.

The status of the card was also recorded on the system, so the representative can tell when it was issued and mailed to the customer. Therefore, the representative in this interaction is able to confidently inform the customer that her card is in the mail. The centralized system means that he could do this without having to delay the customer while checking with other departments for the information.

Question

Which examples demonstrate the benefits of CRM?

Options:

1. CRM systems analyze customer information, which allows companies to adjust their marketing campaigns to suit customers and increase sales

2. CRM allows company representatives at different levels to provide a more efficient and personalized service, which puts the customer at the center of the organization

3. Companies can be sure that they'll never fail in their customer service with CRM systems

4. CRM means not having to have a customer service team

Answer:

Option 1: This option is correct. CRM systems tell companies about the preferences of their customers and allow them to target customers in a more personalized way based on this information.

Option 2: This option is correct. The customer information contained in CRM systems allows employees to make customers feel like they are known personally by the company.

Option 3: This option is incorrect. CRM is extremely useful for storing and analyzing information for better customer service, but it does not prevent the need for effective customer management in other areas of the business.

Option 4: This option is incorrect. It's still important to have trained customer service personnel to give the company a human face.

CRM provides you with systems and processes that put the customer at the center of your organization. CRM helps to close the relationship gap that sometimes exists between a company and its customers, as information can be shared and personalized.

CRM enables customers to feel important as they see the impact that their data has on company policies and processes. For example, customers may log in to a company site and the last products they viewed are remembered and presented. CRM creates a collaborative relationship between the customer and the company.

Marketing processes can be changed as a result of acquiring CRM data. The CRM system knows which products or services your customer purchases and this enables sales teams to cross-sell complementary items. This data also tells you which customers are more profitable.

The bank customer cares only about her personal relationship with the company. She expects the bank to know her when she calls. Because she understands the bank's process, she's ready with her account details. She expects to be given accurate information about her order. The system also allows the representative to enhance the collaborative relationship by making a relevant cross-sell. He offers her a competitive loan as he can see from the system that she has availed of such offers in the past.

CRM provides end-to-end connectivity that links the organization with internal and external customers and suppliers. A complete communication cycle ensures that everyone has timely access to accurate information. A centralized system of up-to-date data keeps information about all of the company's stakeholders flowing in a timely manner throughout the organization. When any one of these stakeholders requires a rapid response to requested information, CRM systems provide this.

The information allows company communications to be directed at the correct audience, in the correct way. The systems provide information that's relevant, convenient, and coherent.

This information can then be acted on as necessary. This makes the processes of a business more transparent and accountable, which helps to retain loyal customers.

Consider the bank example. During a customer service team review, recent customer interactions are analyzed. The team members review this customer's account along with her previous conversations. They notice that she ordered a replacement card, as she lost hers while on vacation. The system automatically adds her into a marketing category for an upcoming offer of vacation insurance and card protection services.

When the customer opts to buy the card protection services and vacation insurance she can immediately view the status of all her current bank products online via her account.

The information provided by the customer led to the bank offering the customer specifically targeted products. The customer can view her relationship with the bank online. Both sides know where they stand in the relationship, as the CRM system is enabling end-to-end connectivity between the customer and the company.

Question

Which examples demonstrate the benefits of CRM?

Options:

1. CRM systems allow you to meet the needs of customers quickly and completely, as they don't have to repeat their details in each interaction

2. CRM systems allow for company representatives to share each customer's relevant data conveniently

3. CRM means that companies don't have to look for feedback on customer preferences

4. CRM is the same process for each company

Answer:

Option 1: This option is correct. The centralized information contained in a CRM system allows employees to see all customer interactions quickly and easily.

Option 2: This option is correct. CRM systems store all customer information in a centralized system, which is easily accessed by company employees.

Option 3: This option is incorrect. Companies with good customer service are always looking for feedback and they use that information to keep their CRM system up-to-date.

Option 4: This option is incorrect. Each company can design and use a CRM that suits its needs and its customers' needs best.

CHAPTER TWO

Creating and Sustaining a Customer-focused Organization

Becoming customer focused

How often have you heard the phrase "the customer is always right"? To succeed in business, you need to recognize the truth behind this phrase. Delivering satisfaction to your customers must be an objective in your business strategy. This brings benefits to your customers and your organization.

A customer-focused strategy is required to ensure that the customer and the company both benefit from the relationship. This strategy enables an organization to handle the customer correctly at every touch point. It helps you gain and retain customers.

In order for customer focus to be successful, a company must carefully organize its functions around customers' needs.

Think of the customer as being at the center of everything you do in your business. Sales, business planning, management policies, purchasing, and everything else should revolve around the customer.

You may have identified issues such as provision of training for staff or financial costs. These are important considerations but each company has its own issues, targets, processes, and customers.

An individual strategy must be devised for every company. Each company's strategy must be aligned with the needs of its own customers.

A customer-focused strategy should contain several key details: why your initiative is of strategic advantage to the business

the overall benefits and how they'll be achieved, and

the level and scope of customer-centricity and the advantage to the company

When developing a customer-focused strategy, organizations need to decide whether they're going to implement a standalone product or a diverse solution.

A standalone product focuses on one area. This product can be software or hardware. An example is customer relationship management, or CRM, software.

A solution bundles together a number of products and services. More robust than a standalone product, it aims to satisfy a variety of customer needs and requests at once. An example would be a combination of CRM software, financial software, and computer hardware.

Question

What key details should a customer-focused strategy include?

Options:

1. How your initiative offers strategic advantage to the company

2. Plans for a customer feedback section within your company web site

Customer Focus

3. The benefits offered and specific details on how they will be achieved

4. What level and scope of customer focus will be used and the advantages of these

5. An outline of the marketing campaign that focuses on your organization's customer centricity

Answer:

Option 1: This option is correct. Your strategy will bring about organization-wide change. Such a major change requires you to demonstrate why it's necessary.

Option 2: This option is incorrect. Web site feedback is a small element of an overall customer-focused strategy, not one of the main aspects.

Option 3: This option is correct. Explaining the benefits and how they will be achieved provides a clear project roadmap for all involved.

Option 4: This option is correct. Identifying the level and scope of customer focus needed means resources will not be wasted. Also, it eliminates the possibility of too little attention being paid to the strategy.

Option 5: This option is incorrect. While a marketing campaign can be an element of an overall strategy, it's not a focal point.

x

Scale and scope of customer focus

A comprehensive customer-focused strategy is built around organization-wide interaction with the customer. When designing the strategy, take into account factors specific to your company and your industry. Issues that must be covered include the scale and scope of the solution needed, the integration requirements for the solution, and the levels of customer focus needed.

Scale and scope requirements revolve around issues such as the number and different kinds of solutions to offer. These solutions are strategically important and can be small, medium, or large depending on the organization and customer-focused strategy involved.

See each size of scale and scope solution to learn more about it.

Small

A small scale and scope solution would involve only a small and non-diverse number of products.

For example, a sound equipment business might have both a physical and an online store. The online store attracts younger customers, while the physical store has mainly customers over 40. The business wants a solution for both outlets that appeals to all ages. A small number of products are needed for such a solution, and a small variety of software and hardware is involved.

Medium

A medium-sized scale and scope solution suits many businesses undergoing a change- management process. A medium solution has more and different kinds of products, as well as a variety of software and hardware.

Consider the example of a call center with several hundred employees that expands to include an after-sales department. A mixture of software, hardware, servers, database, and storage units must now coexist. The solution involves several products, and different types of products so this requires a medium-scale solution.

Large

Large scale and scope solutions are common in major organizations. A great number and variety of products are involved.

For instance, an international insurance company is introducing an organization-wide change of customer service processes. This involves training and assessment to adjust staff behaviors, along with the implementation of various integrated hardware and software systems across continents. This is a large-scale organizational change that calls for a large scale and scope solution.

Claire manages an organization that owns several publishing houses and online publications. The company employs 420 people, operating from different global locations. Claire wants to ensure her company interacts with her customers in an open and transparent manner. Her strategy requires full integration of everyday operations with customer needs in every function. She now must consider what is the best scale and scope solution to implement.

She merges all the organization's financial, sales, and communication systems into one solution. Separate servers and storage facilities from each of the organization's businesses are combined. And an organization-wide toolset is introduced for financial and sales functions.

An integrated communications solution is also introduced. A training system for new software is installed. A large variety of software is blended with the new solution. Also, supplementary hardware is introduced to handle the new demands of the organization. These requirements would be considered large in terms of scale and scope.

Question

David's company specializes in financial training and employs 140 people. The organization provides in-house training events, online courses, financial consultancy services, and software. David wants to reorganize these separate business units to create an organization-wide customer focus. His customer-focused strategy involves the integration of communication channels to create a unified customer experience. Business units will also be reorganized into market segments with responsibility for specific customers.

What is the scale and scope requirement of David's customer-focus solution?

Customer Focus

Options:
1. Small
2. Medium
3. Large

Answer:

Option 1: This option is incorrect. Due to the number of and variety of products involved, a small scale and scope solution would be insufficient.

Option 2: This option is incorrect. The change to customer focus will be organization-wide, so a medium-sized solution wouldn't suffice. Medium scale and scope requirements wouldn't be enough with so many products, systems, and services.

Option 3: This is the correct option. Large scale and scope requirements are necessary. This is due to the vast number of products, services, and software involved in implementing David's customer-focused strategy. Also, the type of services varies across the company.

Integration of customer focus solution

The next part of a customer-focused strategy is deciding on its integration requirements. This refers to the level of integration among the components that make up a customer-focus solution. There are different levels of integration, depending on each organization's individual needs.

The integration requirements for a customer-focus solution can be low, moderate, or high. See each level of integration to learn more about it.

Low

Low integration requirements mean some low-level coordination between solution components is needed. These elements of your business will not be interdependent.

Moderate

Moderate integration involves connecting some different components together. Components can be added

Customer Focus

or replaced at any time without affecting the rest of the system.

High

Organizations have high integration requirements if they have a great number of interdependent components. Many IT companies, for instance, offer software, hardware, and professional services. These elements must operate in an integrated manner.

Consider these examples. Elaine manages an office supplies store. Her stock includes printers, scanners, paper, and ink cartridges. Elaine sources all products from one vendor. She wants a solution where she can combine her ordering and customer relationship management software. This is needed so that staff members can help customers more efficiently. The task of connecting two software programs means a low level of integration is required.

Tom wants his web design software company to address its lack of customer focus. To do this, he'd like to offer a sample program for customers. This program will allow people to choose which software components suit them best. Tom needs this program to be flexible to meet customer expectations. It must allow old components to be deleted and allow new components to be included as they're upgraded. Considering all these factors, Tom's company has moderate integration requirements.

Dennis's mobile communications business is an example of a company with high integration requirements. The company manufactures hardware such as cell phones, tablet devices, and headsets. It also creates software. All cell phone hardware elements must be integrated with the software. In addition, software from other vendors must be incorporated into the cell phone devices. Dennis requires a high-level solution that integrates all these elements together.

Question

In terms of integrating the separate elements of his financial training organization, David has decided to create a modular architecture. This will integrate already interdependent financial, sales, and education software. He wants this modular architecture to allow for the removal of education software if needed.

What degree of integration of the components would be appropriate?

Options:

1. Low
2. Moderate
3. High

Answer:

Option 1: This option is incorrect. There are relatively few software and hardware elements, but they're interdependent.

Option 2: This is the correct option. This change require a moderate degree of integration as it involves bringing separate components together within a modular architecture.

Option 3: This option is incorrect. There's only a certain section of the business that's being integrated – software. As the solution is not extended organization-wide, it wouldn't require a high level of integration.

Levels of customer focus

Organizations face a third key issue when creating a customer-focused strategy: deciding the level of customer focus required. There are three levels of customer focus – low, medium, and high.

Many companies wish to operate with a low level of customer focus. Initially, there's little time or resources devoted to customer focus. However, as this approach develops, there's more customer interaction. There are six steps to achieving a low level of customer focus.

There will be occasional meetings between staff members and customers. Customer needs are grouped with those of business partners.

Expectations of customers are sometimes noted. Also, customer data is infrequently collected and analyzed.

A company's sales spend becomes focused on gaining new customers. Product innovations or developments are flagged through a market push.

Sally's company is an example of having a low level of customer focus. She sells car parts online. Recognizing that the company should be more customer focused, she opted for a low-level approach. While previously she had no contact, she now occasionally meets customers.

During these meetings, she sometimes canvasses opinion on the company web site. To gain new customers, she devotes her marketing spend toward online advertisements.

Question

How often does collection and analysis of customer data occur with a low level of customer focus?

Options:

1. Infrequently
2. Never
3. Often

Answer:

Option 1: This is the correct option. With a low level of customer focus, collection and analysis of customer data occurs infrequently. This just gives you a sense of who your customers are and what they want.

Option 2: This option is incorrect. A customer-focused strategy must include some collection and analysis of customer data.

Option 3: This option is incorrect. A low level of customer focus cannot sustain this approach. At a low level, the resources aren't available to collect and analyze data often.

A medium level of customer focus involves more time and attention, as well as customer involvement. Information gained from customers is given more priority and is actively used.

Customer Focus

There are six steps to take to move to a medium level of customer focus:
- increase the number of customer meetings
- devote attention and focus on customer-related segments of your organization
- use customer data to focus attention on where the company can improve
- assist improvement and innovation through customer input – such as pilot testing
- identify gaps in company performance using customer expectations, and
- devote more funding to organizational development as well as research into the quality and service offered

Chris manages four sports equipment stores. He feels business will improve if the company uses a medium level of customer focus. He focuses on products that customers buy the most and reviews his buying policy on the recommendation of customers.

He doubles his monthly rate of interactions with customers. Data collected shows that rival companies have an interactive element his organization lacks. Chris pilots a project to address this, bringing a sports practice area into his stores.

He devotes funding to developing the store even further to include more interactive elements. Chris also conducts research into the quality of his products and the level of service customers **expect.**

Question

Which statement about a medium level of customer focus is true?

Options:

1. You assist improvement and innovation through customer input such as pilot testing

2. You decrease the number of face-to-face customer meetings

3. You share customer data with rival companies for profit

Answer:

Option 1: This option is correct. Pilot testing is one method of assisting improvement and innovation through customer input. This helps you see which customer-focused initiatives will work.

Option 2: This option is incorrect. When moving to a medium level of customer focus, face-to-face meetings become more prevalent.

Option 3: This option is incorrect. Customer data must be utilized for information on where the company can be improved.

A high level of customer focus means the customer is always a priority. The relationship between the customer and the organization is very close.

Customer-related data becomes a focal point and customers become vital in organizational decisions. There are six steps involved in building a high level of customer focus.

The first step for a high level of customer focus sees the lines blurred between the customers and the company itself. Then, a continuous flow of customer data is utilized. This becomes the basis for operational decisions and business strategies.

Next a high level of customer focus demands you give priority to the expectations of key customer and market segments. Then, you must involve customers in guiding innovations and improvements.

Make sure that customer retention becomes the key investment focus. Finally, competitive benchmarks and market comparisons will now be provided through customer and market gap analysis.

Joanna is the manager of a real estate company and wants to attain a high level of customer focus. The business is divided between a physical office and a well-established web site. The company not only sells homes but provides a gateway for tenants to find rental property.

Their high level of customer focus means Joanna's staff members meet with customers on an almost daily basis. The company now collects data constantly to improve standards and operations. Before any strategic changes, she now consults with customers in detail.

The organization's competitive benchmarks and market comparisons are provided through customer gap analysis. She focuses on retention of customers. Finally, she involves clients in experiments regarding customer-focused innovations and improvements.

Question

David's financial training company has grouped together the needs and expectations of suppliers and customers. He occasionally meets and collects information from customers. Meanwhile, his marketing spend is focused on print advertising to attract new customers.

What level of customer focus is David's company displaying?

Options:
1. Low
2. Medium

3. High

Answer:

Option 1: This is the correct option. David's level of customer focus involves only occasional interaction with the customer. Low-level customer focus groups together the needs of customers with suppliers or partners.

Option 2: This option is incorrect. A medium level of customer focus involves more focus on data and includes more customer interaction. Marketing spend is funneled towards research, development, and improvement.

Option 3: This option is incorrect. For a high level of customer focus, the customer needs to be more involved with the company's decision making. The key focus would be on retention of customers, rather than gaining new customers.

Operational strategies

There are many different operational improvement methodologies available to organizations as they become customer-focused. These methods ensure that the change benefits both the customer and the organization. Two established operational methodologies are Six Sigma and customer relationship management, or CRM.

Six Sigma is based around minimizing variability in manufacturing and business processes. The aim is make these processes error-free. The ideal is to get everything right the first time and every time.

Six Sigma can be adapted to any organization. It identifies the main attributes that have an impact on quality. And it measures the performance of these attributes by collecting data on them. The results are then analyzed to discover where improvements can be made.

With Six Sigma, processes improve and variability is reduced. Organizations save money and time, and can focus more on their customers. These improvements result in higher-quality products and services.

CRM is based around system tools that allow an organization to manage its relationship with customers. A robust CRM system aims to inspire loyalty in an organization's customers.

CRM manages the stages involved in transforming a first-time customer to a loyal customer. It attempts to manage customer behavior after a product or service has been purchased. This can be done through after-sales systems. CRM systems segment customers, highlighting those vital to the company's finances.

Customer opinions and behaviors can be influenced by organizations using CRM. It enables companies to analyze these factors and then develop a strategy that's tailored to the customers' purchasing habits.

Question

Each customer-focused operational strategy has unique characteristics. Match the characteristics to the relevant strategy. Each strategy may have more than one characteristic.

Options:

A. Customer behaviors can be analyzed with this strategy to highlight purchasing habits

B. The strategy can be adapted specifically for each organization that utilizes it

C. This strategy manages the stages involved in a first-time customer becoming a loyal customer

D. Once errors are eliminated from the manufacturing or business processes, this strategy promotes improvement

Targets:

1. CRM

Customer Focus

2. Six Sigma

Answer:

CRM allows for customer behaviors and opinions to be analyzed to highlight purchasing habits. Appealing to these habits can increase customer spending, which is used to create a loyal relationship with new customers.

Six Sigma can adapt to the organization it's applied to. Once adopted, Six Sigma focuses on eliminating errors from the organization's processes.

Managing the strategy

Like any change management process, a customer-focused strategy requires leadership. You need to decide on the level and scope your organization aims to achieve and then you must implement the strategy. This involves planning, consideration, and focus.

There are four key areas that require leadership and management skills. It's a leader's job to see that the transition to customer focus is complete and far-reaching, to generate a sense of urgency and involve key players, to inspire and motivate team members, and to manage any conflict that arises.

See each task to learn more about it.

Ensure that change is complete

A complete and far-reaching customer-focused strategy involves aligning all organizational policies.

Organizational policies often revolve around the company's finances. Managers must tie financial decisions to the customer-focused strategy.

Generate a sense of urgency

Managers need to instill a sense of urgency into an organization-wide customer-focused strategy.

This requires the involvement of the company's key players, who should be central to discussions regarding the change to make them feel part of the process.

Motivate team members

Great leaders inspire and motivate those around them. Managers who can achieve this during a change-management process will benefit greatly.

Serving as a role model helps. Managers must exhibit the type of values and behaviors expected as part of the change.

Manage any conflict

Managing conflict is an inevitable leadership task. For instance, involving the key players in discussions and debates can create tension.

Some will resist change and this needs to be addressed. Strong leaders confront such conflicts and find a resolution.

Transforming your company doesn't end with a manager's responsibilities. In most cases, managers are supported by an implementation team.

Your implementation team is responsible for transforming the organization. Good communication skills are needed, as the group will work with different sections of the company and various job levels. Members of this team must be considered influential within their particular section.

Assigning tasks within the implementation team is a delicate process. The group should hold a frank and honest initial meeting. Each member should be assigned a specific task. Ultimately, completing the task is each individual's responsibility but delegation of activities must be within the power of implementation team members.

Question

What are the duties of a leader when implementing customer focus within an organization?

Options:

1. Defer solving conflict issues between team members until after customer focus is implemented

2. Generate a sense of urgency and involve the key players

3. Inspire and motivate team members

4. Assign ultimate responsibility for customer focus to someone else

5. Manage any conflict that arises

6. Concentrate solely on getting key players to promote the customer-focused strategy

7. Ensure change is complete and far reaching

Answer:

Option 1: This option is incorrect. Conflict issues must be resolved in order for the implementation of customer focus to work.

Option 2: This option is correct. Generating a sense of urgency and involving the key players means the strategy will be implemented as quickly as possible.

Option 3: This option is correct. Exhibiting the values and behaviors expected from the process is leading by example. This type of leadership encourages employees to follow their management.

Option 4: This option is incorrect. Leaders must assume ultimate responsibility for implementing customer focus.

Customer Focus

Option 5: This option is correct. Management must resolve issues or conflicts related to those resisting the change management process.

Option 6: This option is incorrect. Gaining the support of key players for customer focus is important. However, it shouldn't be the only matter a leader concentrates on.

Option 7: This option is correct. Generating a sense of urgency and involving the key players means the strategy will be implemented as quickly as possible.

Promote the strategy

Implementing a customer-focused strategy involves three main stages: promoting the strategy, education and training, and improving processes.

Promoting the strategy involves building awareness by introducing a pilot project. You must engender ownership of the strategy among employees. Also, you need to conduct formal surveys of your customers.

See each stage of promoting the strategy for more information.

Build awareness

Employees will want to know the benefits of change, so build awareness. One common method of introducing a new concept is through a pilot program.

Find a section of your business that – in terms of functionality and size – is typical of the organization. Pilot the approach to customer focus within this part of the organization.

Engender ownership

Customer Focus

An organization's first market is its staff members. They must feel part of any strategic change.

Help this process by introducing an employee feedback system on new strategies. Encourage employees to take part.

Conduct formal surveys

Gaining knowledge of customer needs and expectations is essential. One way of getting this knowledge is through formal surveys.

Varieties of surveys include telephone interviews, mail satisfaction surveys, face-to-face interviews, e-mail surveys, complaint-analysis tools, lost-account surveys, focus groups, and comment cards.

Jane and Steve work for a consumer electronics organization. Jane manages the organization's sales team, while Steve manages IT innovation. Jane and Steve are members of a team that is implementing a customer-focused strategy.

Follow along as Jane and Steve discuss various problems regarding how to promote their organization's customer-focused strategy.

Jane: My team doesn't seem to believe customer-focus is of any benefit.

Jane is confused.

Steve: Perhaps they don't feel involved in the process. Maybe you could volunteer the Sales section of the company for the customer-focus pilot project?

Jane: Another part of the company is being used for the pilot project. What about giving my team members ownership? What methods would you use to get them on board that way?

Jane is still a little confused.

Steve: I would introduce a system where your staff members can give feedback. Encourage everyone to take part.

Jane: Good idea. How are things going for you at the customer end?

Jane is happy her problem is solved.

Steve: Well, we're reaching current customers with surveys but I'd like to know why previous customers left. Investigating old e-mail complaints is taking up too much time.

Steve is slightly irritated.

Jane: What about surveying former customers? Track down clients we've lost over time and send a survey to them. Ask why they don't do business with us anymore.

Steve: That could work. I'll delegate that task to one of my team members. Thanks!

Steve is pleased.

Jane and Steve's actions are intended to promote the organization's customer-focused strategy. Steve's suggestion of an employee feedback system will help get employee buy-in for the strategy.

Meanwhile, Jane's idea of surveying old customers will help promote the strategy. Speaking to alienated customers can help rectify outstanding issues.

Question

A DVD rental chain is implementing a customer-focused strategy across the organization. Which are examples of how the company could market the strategy?

Options:

1. Build awareness by introducing a pilot project in one DVD store

2. Test the strategy among the boardroom-level implementation group
3. Study how similar strategies are marketed in other DVD rental chains
4. Engender ownership among employees by involving them in the process
5. Conduct formal surveys of customers who come into the DVD stores

Answer:

Option 1: This option is correct. Building awareness by introducing a pilot scheme helps promote the advantages of becoming customer focused. If one part of the organization quantifiably benefits from change, the remainder follows suit.

Option 2: This option is incorrect. Your implementation group is too invested in the change to be a test group.

Option 3: This option is incorrect. While studying similar strategies is of benefit, this would be done at the preparation stage of a strategy.

Option 4: This option is correct. Engendering ownership among employees addresses the needs of your staff members. They must feel involved in any strategic change.

Option 5: This option is correct. By conducting formal surveys of your customers, you'll be able to find out their expectations.

Educate and train

A customer-focused strategy cannot work without an educated workforce. This involves two tasks: holding meetings and training employees.

Both all-company and smaller meetings are good ideas when trying to instill a new organizational concept. All-company meetings are an expedient way to get the message across about customer focus.

A series of smaller meetings can be very effective. Your implementation team can lead meetings with their sections of the organization. Continue these meetings until every employee is informed of the organization's new strategy.

Not every employee is a natural when it comes to customer focus. Some need direction to meet the standards your strategy aspires to. Training all employees on the organization's new approach to customers is recommended.

Customer Focus

Training should give frontline and backroom staff the customer-focus skills to deal with any situation. It should focus on being responsive to customers. All employees should gain organization-oriented problem-solving skills during training.

Dealing with customer needs and complaints must be focal points. In addition, organization managers must be trained in customer-focused service management.

Remember Jane and Steve? They have concerns over employee adaptation to the customer focus strategy. Follow along as they discuss ways to inform and train the employees.

Steve: I'm worried about how to inform staff members about the strategy. We agreed to introduce the customer-focused strategy with an all-company meeting. However, it's difficult to get everyone in the same building at once.

Steve is concerned.

Jane: That's been mentioned to me. Perhaps we can have a series of smaller meetings instead? Maybe each section of the company can hold an individual meeting?

Jane sounds concerned

Steve: That's far more realistic. How are preparations for the company-wide training program?

Steve is happy his problem is solved.

Jane: Some individuals seem to feel they don't need it. They feel they're already customer focused.

Jane is worried.

Steve: The way to handle that is to explain that we need everyone operating at the same skill level. Some people have natural customer skills, some don't.

Steve is positive

Jane: Thanks! I'll make that point to them.

Jane is happy.

Jane and Steve's issues over employee adaptation to the strategy are common ones. Many companies have difficulty organizing all-company meetings.

The issue about staff members who feel they don't need training is another key point. This must be addressed so the organization can be sure each employee has adequate training.

Question

A restaurant chain with eight outlets is concerned about its level of customer focus. The company has decided to implement a customer-focused strategy. Which are examples of how the company could educate and train its workforce on the strategy?

Options:

1. Create an organization-wide multiple-choice questionnaire on customer focus

2. Hold a series of small meetings – one in each restaurant

3. Hold an organization-wide meeting, chaired by the CEO, inviting all staff members from all restaurants

4. Implement a series of regular team-building exercises on all-company day trips

5. Create an organization-wide service training program that will be run in each restaurant

Answer:

Option 1: This option is incorrect. Such a questionnaire can be of benefit when building a customer-focused strategy. However, the questionnaire has no far-reaching impact by itself.

Option 2: This option is correct. Holding a series of small meetings across the organization will help spread the word about customer focus. Employees learn about the importance of the customer from the manager they report to.

Option 3: This option is correct. An organization-wide meeting quickly and effectively gets the point across. In addition, having a senior member of staff chairing the meeting emphasizes its importance.

Option 4: This option is incorrect. While the implementation of team-building exercises can have a positive impact, they're not suitable in this instance. They lack the requisite elements for educating or training staff.

Option 5: This option is correct. Creating an organization-wide service training program is a great way to educate and train employees. It should give all levels of staff the ability to deal with any customer-focused situation.

Improve processes

The final stage in implementing a customer-focused strategy centers on improving processes. This is achieved in three ways: you adopt a continuous improvement program, you review all company processes and procedures, and you design and implement standards for service excellence.

Involving employees in a continuous improvement program helps engender a feeling of ownership. You should establish a process where employees actually lead customer-focus activities. This utilizes their frontline experience with customers.

Employees can lead through a variety of initiatives. They can establish groups that work on customer- focused service and product quality.

A series of process-improvement brainstorming sessions involving employees should become a regular feature. Also, teams that focus on process-improvement tasks should be established.

Customer Focus

Improving customer-focused processes and procedures within an organization, requires an in-depth review of key systems. Various systems may need redesign. These include telephone and computer systems, accounting and payment systems, web site user interface, and e-mail services. Also possibly affected are customer relationship management (CRM) systems, ordering and sales systems, and post-
sales services. As well, you should consider the impact on crisis and contingency solutions, logistics and supply systems, accounting systems, payment systems, and customer-complaint services.

Only by designing standards for service excellence can quality customer service be achieved. These standards must then be implemented.

Examples of standards that help promote customer focus include a set deadline for responses to e-mail inquiries. Also, the maximum number of rings before a phone is answered should be established.

In addition, a fixed deadline for filling all orders can be useful. Setting a maximum time limit for returning all customer calls is also a popular strategy.

Jane and Steve are finalizing their customer-focused strategy. Follow along as they discuss ways of improving processes.

Jane: Steve, which of the company's procedures and systems need to be redesigned?

Steve: We need to redesign our customer complaints and post-sales systems. They don't address the needs of customers to the correct standards.

Steve sounds upbeat.

Jane: In terms of customer complaints, what's the first step to providing better service?

Jane is relaxed about the situation.

Steve: I think first of all, we need to have a deadline allotted for responses to e-mails. This covers complaints, as well as general e-mails.

Steve is positive.

Jane: Good idea. But, I'm still having an issue getting my staff members on board. While they've agreed to training, they don't feel involved in the process.

Jane is concerned.

Steve: I think putting them at the forefront of implementing the organization's continuous-improvement program will help. Along with employees from different sections of the organization, they can drive that forward.

Steve sounds upbeat.

Jane: Excellent! I'll start by establishing a team to focus on process- improvement tasks.

Jane is happy.

It's imperative that Jane and Steve consider which processes and procedures need to be redesigned. This helps drive the company's customer service forward.

In addition, the pair are working on designing customer-focused standards. They're making sure customer focus reaches every part of the organization.

Question

A large clothing web site is unsure it's offering customers enough attention. A decision has been made to implement a customer-focused strategy.

Which are examples of how the company could improve processes when implementing the strategy?

Options:

1. Involve customers in a survey on improving processes
2. Review financial implications of implementing a customer-focused strategy
3. Implement an employee-centered continuous improvement program for web site and call center staff
4. Design and implement standards for service excellence throughout the company
5. Review major procedures and processes including the company web site, phone systems, and sales software

Answer:

Option 1: This option is incorrect. Involving customers at this point is not necessary. It's an internal element of the change management process, not the implementation of the strategy.

Option 2: This option is incorrect. The company's finances should be reviewed at the outset of this process. This is not the focus of improving processes.

Option 3: This option is correct. Implementing an employee-centered continuous improvement program is key. The people dealing with customers will directly help improve processes.

Option 4: This option is correct. Designing and implementing standards for service excellence will improve customer experience and create standard work practices.

Option 5: This option is correct. Reviewing procedures and processes vital to the company is key to process review. It highlights which procedures or processes must be improved or redesigned.

Case Study: Question 1 of 3
Scenario:

For your convenience, the case study is repeated with each question.

Jason, the manager of a telecommunications company, has decided to implement an organization-wide customer-focused strategy.

Question:

Before taking any further steps, Jason realizes that there's one crucial first step to be taken. What is it?

Options:

1. Ask his implementation team to test the strategy on an individual basis

2. Make sure he knows what his customers and staff members think of the strategy

3. Review and improve processes such as the web site user interface and telephone systems

Answer:

Option 1: This option is incorrect. This would not be necessary as a pilot project is already in place. It is also too varied of a group of employees for a robust pilot project.

Option 2: This is the correct option. Knowing what your customers and staff members think of the strategy is crucial. You engender ownership of the strategy among staff members by including their opinions in the process. You can garner opinions through formal surveys.

Option 3: This option is incorrect. A pilot project has already been implemented to showcase the strategy's potential within the organization.

Case Study: Question 2 of 3

What should have been done before a program of training and development was initiated?

Options:

1. A survey of employees about whether they feel training is necessary
2. Customer-focused software should be installed across the organization
3. A company-wide meeting to introduce the initiative should be held

Answer:

Option 1: This option is incorrect. While some staff members may feel they don't need training, levels of knowledge must be similar organization-wide.

Option 2: This option is incorrect. The training and development process prepares staff for any new software needed. So training should come first.

Option 3: This is the correct option. A company-wide meeting prepares staff for the change to customer focus. It is the quickest way to get across the importance of the initiative.

Case Study: Question 3 of 3

The company put in place an employee-centered continuous improvement program.

What else could the company do during this phase of implementing the strategy?

Options:

1. Implement standards for dealing with all customer e-mails
2. Disregard all previous standards for answering phones
3. Redesign the product portfolio
4. Put in place standards for answering phones
5. Redesign the after-sales service systems

Answer:

Option 1: This option is correct. By putting in place standards for dealing with e-mails, both employees and customers know where they stand. A customer can have a certain expectation for an answer to an e-mail. And an employee knows the amount of time needed to find an answer to the customer query.

Option 2: This option is incorrect. If the company has any previous standards for answering phones these should be redesigned.

Option 3: This option is incorrect. A redesign of a company's product portfolio may be a result of customer focus. However, it will not occur at this stage in the strategy's development.

Option 4: This option is correct. Putting in place standards for answering phones helps customers and employees. Employees will make sure to address customer queries via phone in an expedient manner.

Option 5: This option is correct. Redesigning an after-sales service helps many companies when becoming customer focused. Better relationships create loyal customers.

Customer-focus implementation issues

Implementing a customer-focused strategy is not without its challenges. These must be navigated for your strategy to be sustainable. This requires constant attention but there are several advantages to achieving a sustainable solution.

Take the example of James, the manager of a large software company that adopted a customer- focused strategy two years ago. Anton, a new sales manager, is not convinced of the benefits of customer focus. James decides Anton must understands the concept's benefits in order to work productively.

James breaks down the advantages of sustained customer focus into three sections. First, he explains that sustainable customer focus allows the organization to build long-term revenue. He reveals that customer loyalty is stronger since implementing the strategy.

James explains that a sustained customer-focused strategy attracts new customers. By listening to customer needs and expectations the company can tailor services to them. James notes that this attracts new customers.

Finally, he reveals that customer focus brings out the best in employees. This is achieved by creating a sense of employee buy-in through various initiatives.

Question

What are the advantages of being able to sustain customer focus?

Options:

1. You build long-term revenue
2. You will be able to stop spending money on promotion efforts
3. You attract new customers
4. You bring out the best in your employees
5. You only have to focus on your most desirable customers

Answer:

Option 1: This option is correct. You'll be able to build long term revenue through loyal customers. This occurs through high levels of customer focus.

Option 2: This option is incorrect. Your customer-focused strategy may help drive customer loyalty, but you will still have to expend resources on promoting your organization to your target audiences.

Option 3: This option is correct. You'll attract new customers though sustained customer focus. New customers will learn from others about your level of customer focus.

Option 4: This option is correct. You'll bring out the best in your employees as customer focus standards are adopted. Sustaining customer focus takes constant work – this has to be done by dedicated employees.

Option 5: This option is incorrect. Customer-focus strategies only remain sustainable if you focus on the needs of every customer.

Though there are great advantages, sustainable customer focus doesn't happen easily. Any change management process will bring up unexpected issues. Indeed, difficulties are common after the strategy is launched and initial enthusiasm has died down.

A number of issues can arise post-launch of an organization wide customer-focused strategy:
- there is a lack of management buy-in for the strategy,
- the customer service strategy is not defined nor is there any common understanding about its objectives,
- service quality is not integrated into the company,
- the organization does not listen to its customers, and
- customer focus is not blended into the training and development process.

See each of the common post-launch issues for more information.

Lack of management buy-in

Those in management positions must keep their commitment to customer focus. Their attention to customer satisfaction must stay at the same level from the start.

There's a danger of senior managers ignoring customer focus for more familiar business concerns. Some may view the strategy as having only short-term gains. In turn, they can hand responsibility for customer service over to a subordinate.

Strategy is not defined

Your customer-focused strategy must be clearly defined. Advantages of the process must be unambiguous. The strategy's objectives across the organization must be communicated on a sustained basis.

Service quality is not integrated

If quality customer service isn't integrated into the organization, the new philosophy cannot flourish. Customer focus should be evident at every touch point of the business. If it's not, and it fails to halt previous bad habits, the strategy may encounter serious issues.

Organization not listening to customers

During the change management process that leads to customer focus, organizations can forget to listen to customers. Management and employees may still feel it's a case of "us and them," the organization versus the customer.

However, the change means helping the customer and, in turn, helping the organization. A relationship between both parties must be fostered.

Customer focus not blended into training and development

An organization-wide training and development program is crucial from the outset. It can't be a one-off thing though. Customer focus must be blended into the training and development process of the organization permanently. Integrate it into every facet of company training and evaluation.

Question

Match each post-launch issue to a possible solution to the issue.

Options:

Customer Focus

A. Customer focus is not blended into the training and development process

B. A lack of management buy-in for the strategy

C. The organization is not listening to its customers

D. Service quality is not integrated into the organization

Targets:

1. Employees should have frequent and up-to-date training on customer focus

2. Those in management positions demonstrate their 100% commitment to customer focus

3. The relationship between the organization and the customer is nurtured

4. Customer focus is evident at every touch point of the organization

Answer:

Training programs on customer focus should not be allowed to be a once-off. Employees should have consistent and up-to-date training on customer focus. Customer focus touches every facet of the organization and so recurrent training is a requisite to its success.

Those in management positions must keep a consistent focus on customer focus. Deflecting their responsibilities sets a poor example to employees. A successful customer-centric strategy needs management-level buy-in.

A relationship between the organization and the customer must be fostered. This relationship must involve feedback from the customer.

Customer focus must be evident at every touch point of the organization. This way a high quality of service will be integrated across the company.

Management support

There's no point in undertaking a change-management process unless it's sustainable. There are four factors involved in ensuring this strategy is sustainable: management support, recognition and rewards, training and development, and reviewing progress.

Management support is essential to help focus your organization around the customer. This leadership engenders sustained customer focus and long-term success. It requires time and energy, as well as decisive action and ongoing communication.

There are six management support tasks associated with sustaining customer focus within an organization:
- integrating service excellence into all management activities,
- ensuring the customer-focused strategy has clear definition and is communicated properly,
- seeking out disgruntled customers before they have a chance to complain,

- setting effective service goals,
- assigning explicit accountability to all, and
- defining service boundaries.

See each management task for more information.

Integrating service excellence

Management must be consistent with regards to customer focus. Service excellence gives a competitive advantage to any organization using it.

A loyal customer relationship has service excellence at its root. Customers return to organizations where service excellence is standard.

Ensuring strategy has clear definition

Defining a clear path by which your strategy can be successful helps employees. They are your first audience – you must communicate your customer focus vision to them.

Define both goals and guidelines for employees. Communicate exactly how these goals and guidelines will help service quality.

Seeking out disgruntled customers

Seeking out disgruntled customers before they have a chance to complain is a very proactive move.

Such action indicates that you understand the customer's concerns. It's then easier to build your relationship with them based on this understanding.

Setting effective service goals

Setting effective service goals means all employees are aware of exactly what's expected of them.

Service goals should be clearly set out, telling employees exactly what their responsibilities are. These responsibilities should be both achievable and measurable.

Assigning explicit accountability

Assigning explicit accountability to everyone within the organization plays a vital role in keeping customer focus sustainable.

Your customer-focused strategy requires the organization to work together. Everyone must know exactly what their responsibilities are.

Defining service boundaries

As part of clearly defining the customer focus, service boundaries must be highlighted.

For example, it must be communicated how these boundaries will assist service quality. Knowledge of service boundaries will assist employees when assessing any deviations from routine service.

Question

What are examples of how customer focus can be sustained in an organization through management support?

Options:

1. Management clearly defines service boundaries to all employees, outlining what's expected of them

2. Management assigns explicit accountability to management-level employees only

3. Management begins a process of seeking out unhappy customers before they have a chance to complain

4. Management decides which systems to change as a result of the customer-focused strategy 5. Management assigns explicit accountability to all employees throughout the organization

Answer:

Option 1: This option is correct. A definition of service boundaries means that expectations of employees are

Customer Focus

clearly communicated. Maintaining these boundaries leads to a sustainable customer-focused strategy.

Option 2: This option is incorrect. Management must assign accountability throughout the organization. Leaving only those at the management level accountable for sustaining customer focus will create difficulties. Employees may feel they don't have to do anything to sustain customer focus. This can derail the entire customer-focused strategy.

Option 3: This option is correct. Management should seek out disgruntled customers before they have a chance to complain. Changing an organization's processes and procedures has an effect on the customer. Reaching out to explain why this change is happening helps ease their transition. This will help the organization keep those customers in the long term.

Option 4: This option is incorrect. This decision will be made in advance of deciding how to sustain customer focus. Deciding which systems to change occurs between the planning and implementation stages of the strategy.

Option 5: This option is correct. Explicitly making every employee accountable means they realize what's expected individually to sustain customer focus.

Recognition and rewards

Sustaining customer focus throughout an organization takes a lot of hard work. Recognizing and rewarding this hard work is also key. By using various recognition and reward programs, management can motivate employees and build commitment to customer focus.

Different factors make up a successful recognition and reward system. Consider the example of Monique. Her gaming hardware company has implemented a customer-focused strategy.

She has instilled a policy of positive reinforcement through formal recognition of effort in her company. Rewards and recognition follow goals met by an individual or team. If specific targets are achieved, Monique rewards employees in a recognizable manner.

Monique created a system for acknowledging and rewarding employees for good customer service. This involved defining the criteria for good customer service. To help highlight good customer service, there's a

Customer Focus

nomination process among team members for various rewards. Customer feedback is also used to recognize those who demonstrate high levels of customer focus. A bonus system that's explicitly measured by employees attaining certain goals is also introduced.

Rewards related to customer focus can vary greatly. Take Damien's insurance company for example.

Rewards in his organization can be simple recognition, symbols, or tokens or even tangible rewards. Simple recognition can mean a manager congratulating an employee on a job well done. Symbols or tokens can range from certificates to a change in title. Tangible rewards can include money, merchandise, or even trips.

Damien also concentrates on conducting performance evaluations. For these evaluations, he measures performance against established customer-focused service standards. He makes sure that rewards are based around achieving, or going beyond these standards.

Damien has developed a motivated workforce. This will be of long-term benefit to the company, as well as the customer.

Question

What are examples of how customer focus can be sustained in an organization through recognition and rewards?

Options:

1. Conduct a prize draw that includes employees across the organization

2. Utilize established service standards by conducting performance evaluations

3. Offer a variety of rewards to employees for meeting certain goals

4. Define good customer service then operate a system for acknowledging and rewarding employees meeting these standards

5. Have a nomination system where employees failing to meet service standards are pinpointed every month

Answer:

Option 1: This option is incorrect. This type of reward is not based on the right criteria. Recognition and rewards must come from goals that have been achieved. A prize draw means the winner is chosen regardless of customer focus efforts.

Option 2: This option is correct. Conducting performance evaluations using established service standards is vital. Performance must be assessed by recognized standards to be effective. This will keep performance aligned with customer focus.

Option 3: This option is correct. Varying levels of rewards clearly indicates the level of achievement involved. Certain levels of customer focus are rewarded with verbal congratulations and others with money. This sets out the hierarchy of rewards offered for customer service. It shows employees what they can expect for their efforts.

Option 4: This option is correct. A system for acknowledging and rewarding employees for good customer service is of great advantage. Only by achieving the goal of good customer service can acknowledgement and reward come. An established system means every employee knows what's required to gain that acknowledgement or reward.

Option 5: This option is incorrect. Recognition and rewards are based around positive reinforcement rather than negative feedback. Performance evaluations will pinpoint those not meeting their goals. Therefore, there's no need for other employees to get involved in this process.

Training and development

A customer-focused strategy requires an initial effort to educate and train a workforce. However, sustaining customer focus is about continuous training and skills development. Customer service needs to be integrated into all ongoing training programs.

There are some key training and development steps to be taken to sustain customer focus within an organization:
- constantly renew customer focus training,
- provide training and development for all levels,
- offer a self-development program to all employees,
- organize a recruitment process which focuses on customer-mindedness,
- develop a program of coaching and facilitation for managers, and
- integrate learning into the workplace via work-based activities.

See the steps of training and development to sustain customer focus for more details on each.

Renew customer focus training

An effective customer-focused strategy needs to be constantly renewed.

An example of how to achieve this is by conducting a training needs analysis. Doing so regularly results in new training needs being identified. Trainers must be kept updated on the customer-focus initiative's progress.

Train all levels

From senior management to new employees, training and development must be supplied at all levels. This means every full-time and part-time employee must receive customer-focus training.

For example, every employee will need sufficient product training and managers will need leadership training.

Offer self-development program

Offering all employees a program of self-development will be beneficial organization-wide. This can involve qualifications or certificates in customer focus being offered to employees via the program.

For example, an employee should be encouraged to learn more about customer expectations. By offering the reward of a qualification for this process you motivate the employee.

Organize recruitment process

New recruits to the organization must be in tune with your customer-focused strategy. In order to ensure this, you must organize a recruitment process that focuses on customer-mindedness.

For example, as part of this process, make new recruits aware of your strategy. Also, integrate customer focus into any induction programs.

Develop coaching for managers

Providing a program of coaching and facilitation skills to managers will empower them.

Managers must be coached in training techniques, as it encourages them to provide on-the-job training.

Integrate learning into the workplace

Integrating learning into the workplace via work-based activities can be very effective. There are several approaches to this.

For example, you can use audio or video recordings of employees displaying various levels of customer focus. You can also do the same to examine competitors' customer focus. In addition, you can provide team-building events and training.

Question

What are examples of how customer focus can be sustained in an organization through training and development?

Options:

1. Developing a program of coaching and facilitation for managers to empower them

2. Integrating learning into the workplace via work-based activities such as team-building exercises

3. Developing standard "holidays" from customer focus so that each employee takes a break from the strategy

4. Developing a regular customer-focus exam for your implementation team

5. Constantly renewing customer focus training through initiatives like training needs analysis

Customer Focus

Answer:

Option 1: This option is correct. Customer focus requires developing a program of coaching and facilitation for managers. Managers must feel empowered within a customer-focused strategy, which coaching and facilitation provides.

Option 2: This option is correct. Integrating learning into the workplace via work-based activities is of benefit to all employees. Staff can learn from practical examples of customer focus.

Option 3: This option is incorrect. Employees must continue to develop their customer-focus skills. This requires training and on-the-job learning. There is no benefit from taking a break from customer focus as it's at the heart of any successful organization.

Option 4: This option is incorrect. An exam may be beneficial to ascertain the knowledge level of your implementation team but it puts pressure on employees and is not a good way to encourage customer focus.

Option 5: This option is correct. Constantly renewing customer-focus training will keep it up-to-date with customer-focus trends. This helps sustain a customer-centric strategy.

Reviewing progress

A customer-focused strategy must evolve. Sustainable strategies include regular process reviews that help to focus attention on which elements are working and which are not. These reviews should indicate whether the original objectives are being achieved and ascertain customer reactions to the new strategy.

Dylan is a partner in a medium-sized mobile communications company. The company has implemented a customer-focused strategy. However, he is worried about the progress. He decides a review is needed and bases this around five main tasks.

First Dylan reviews the progress of a quality initiative at regular intervals. This measures whether original objectives have been achieved. It checks if key criteria have been met, what priorities should be addressed, and what the disappointments are so far.

Dylan begins monitoring the metrics that matter most to customers and staff. These metrics are what are considered the important elements of Dylan's organization. He surveys both groups on the subject. Monitoring these factors on an ongoing basis leads to a sustainable customer-focused strategy.

Dylan starts to use customer relationship management (CRM) techniques to review customer-focus progress. Dylan notes that CRM techniques can help in monetary terms – identifying the most profitable target customers. Using CRM techniques, his organization can tailor its services to meet customers' needs.

Measuring customer satisfaction on a regular basis is central to any sustainable customer-focused strategy. Dylan's organization uses several methods including focus groups and panels with customers. Customers are asked to identify which sections of the organization can be improved upon.

Dylan sends questionnaires to his employees and customers. Telephone and Internet surveys are undertaken with both groups. Customer satisfaction surveys and employee attitude surveys are conducted. Dylan makes sure that all employees receive feedback from these surveys.

Question

What are examples of how customer focus can be sustained in an organization through reviewing progress?

Options:

1. Initiate a process where measuring customer satisfaction is done on a regular basis

2. Send questionnaires to managers that focus on strategic benefits of customer focus

3. Initiate a process where you measure customer satisfaction on an infrequent basis

4. Having acquired customer relationship management (CRM) systems, employ the software's various techniques

5. Begin an initiative where your organization sends questionnaires to internal as well as external customers

Answer:

Option 1: This option is correct. Measuring customer satisfaction on a regular basis is the center of reviewing progress. The customer is the center of your organization. If they are not satisfied, both the customer and the organization suffer.

Option 2: This option is incorrect. This point in the process is about reviewing the strategy that has been put in place. Strategic benefits of customer focus are covered in the original strategy.

Option 3: This option is incorrect. For a customer-focused strategy to be sustainable, it must regularly assess customer satisfaction. Infrequent measurement of customer satisfaction will prove insufficient for improving customer focus.

Option 4: This option is correct. Using CRM techniques can help your organization offer what customers need and expect. By using the available techniques you can pinpoint which customers are beneficial to the organization.

Option 5: This option is correct. By sending questionnaires to internal and external customers, you are reviewing progress from all angles. Employee and customer concerns must be aired in order to sustain progress of your customer-focused strategy.

CHAPTER THREE

Customer-focused Interaction

Using social media

The traditional definition of customer service has been blurred by the explosion of social media. New ways to achieve positive customer-focused interactions mean customer service is no longer about simply servicing your customers – it's also about promoting your company to the world.

In order to stay current, your company must recognize the benefits of using customer-focused interaction technologies and social media. If you can, your company will benefit from providing a new form of excellent customer service.

There are many social media applications your customers may be using – everything from posts on blogs or company forums, to posting photos or videos, to profile status updates on social networking web sites.

A few of the most familiar social media applications include Facebook, Twitter, LinkedIn, and Talkbiznow.

Customers are having conversations about products over the Internet whether companies know it or not. It's the companies' responsibility to become engaged in the conversation. So you should be familiar with a few ways social media can be used in customer service, such as to communicate with customers, leverage customer loyalty, and address customer concerns.

See each use of social media in customer service to learn more.

Communicate with customers

Social media can be used to monitor customer comments but it can also feed customers selected information. For example, social media can help track customer complaints, highlight loyal customers, or give customers special offers.

Social media can also help personalize business transactions. Customers often want to talk with another human being, be it someone from the company or another customer. If someone's there to listen and respond, customers feel a more personal connection.

Leverage customer loyalty

Social media can also be used to broadcast customer loyalty in order to promote a business or product. By closely watching customers' conversations and comments, you can highlight those that help promote the company.

But, while social media can be used to broadcast good customer feedback, the downside is it can also spread negative feedback just as quickly.

As a result, companies need to have strategies in place that help promote and generate more positive feedback and at the same time, helps contain or curtail any negative customer feedback from social media sites to gain more loyal customers.

Address customer concerns

Using social media to help address customer concerns can be an extension of the company's service process. Social media interactions in real time can allow for more immediate responses and back and forth conversation.

Also, companies can provide self-service through social media with customers answering other customers' questions. Concerns can be addressed easily through additional instructions, troubleshooting, past logged issues, or FAQs posted by customers for customers.

It's important to note that using social media in customer service isn't a cure-all. It's become a necessity for companies but the learning curve is steep. Most companies don't know how to handle complaints through this medium. Rules for using social media to support customer service don't exist, and it's a broad area to monitor and respond to. Also, social media for customer service isn't your typical customer service interface with business hours – there isn't always someone there to respond.

Advantages of social media

Once your business takes steps to start using social media in customer-focused service, you'll begin to notice the advantages. And those advantages are not just for your business but also for your customers.

Using social media to communicate with customers allows your customers to feel they're being heard. And this results in two benefits – it deepens the business-customer relationship and provides customers with immediate satisfaction.

See each benefit to learn more.

Deepens the relationship

Social media gives customers a voice and visible proof that their comments are being read and acted upon. If the company is seen as reaching out to customers, this works to deepen relationships.

Using social media switches the power to the customers, especially when a self-service option is available. But this power also enables customers to post complaints for all to read. Companies have to adapt their customer service responses accordingly. And when everything's going well, companies can use positive comments to boost their image.

Provides immediate satisfaction

Using social media to address concerns is advantageous to customers as they get immediate satisfaction. Often they can choose between real-time chats, forum replies, or instant technical help from customer service representatives or other customers. And spending less money on wages or content creation while still pleasing your customers is a benefit to your business as well.

Consider this example. An online ticketing company has a system to gather customer information through social media. When customers create a membership they enter personal details. As well, the events they search for and buy tickets to are tracked as their personal preferences. Then, when customers log onto the ticketing site the next time, they receive information and suggestions for events that may interest them. Customer queries are also answered instantaneously.

This cycle of gathering information is ongoing. Every time a customer logs on or posts a question or comment, this information is recorded.

So having those personal details constantly change and expand deepens the relationship with those loyal customers. People begin to feel that the organization, or ticketing company, understands their wants and needs and is making an effort to please them. They begin to feel like people, not just numbers.

As well, whether customers e-mail customer service or post a question to the company forum, they're able to

Customer Focus

receive a quick response through social media. Being able to provide immediate customer satisfaction, getting back to customers quickly with the information they're looking for, is a real benefit.

Question

Consider your organization. How well do you think your business is communicating with your customers?

Options:

1. Not very well
2. Moderately well
3. Well
4. Very well

Answer:

Option 1: You indicated that your business doesn't communicate very well with customers. You might consider employing some type of social media to reach out to your customers. Using social media to communicate with customers can result in two benefits – deepening the business-customer relationship and providing customers with immediate satisfaction.

Option 2: You indicated that your business communicates moderately well with customers. You might consider exploring more social media options to expand on what your business is doing currently. When you use social media to communicate with customers, you deepen the relationship and are better able to give customers what they need.

Option 3: You indicated that your business communicates well with customers. You've probably already implemented some type of social media into your customer service strategy. Remember, in being better able to gather information, you're then better able to give customers what they want. This will result in more loyal and happy customers.

Option 4: You indicated that your business communicates very well with customers. Congratulations, your business is well on its way to meeting customer requirements. Don't forget to continue to explore what social media can do to help you gather information and communicate with your customers.

Besides the advantages to customers, companies can benefit from using social media in customer service too.

Companies can get competitive insights by monitoring their competition within the social media realm. Customers use social media to make comments and share likes and dislikes about products and services. So if you're monitoring discussions or feedback your competition is receiving, you're also gaining information about what customers want.

You might also be able to lure competitors' customers over to your company. You can provide special deals or offers based on competitive insights. This way your company can learn from competitors' mistakes and wins.

For example, a food manufacturer was monitoring its competitor's customer feedback forum. The manufacturer noticed customers were making complaints about a product similar to one it was about to release. This competitive insight allowed it to delay the release of the new product in order to take a different approach. It used details from the customers' complaints on the forum to change the packaging slightly and create a new strategy for release.

Besides gaining competitive insight, social media can also give businesses insight into its customer base. Every point of contact made through social media provides businesses with more information about the customers who are using it.

So if you know which customers use certain social networking sites most frequently, you can create custom differentiated demographical experiences aimed at different groups, such as age groups.

You can use the customer information you have, and the social media available, to reach select groups of customers with specific deals or branding.

So think back to the food manufacturer example. Based on the information gathered, the manufacturer knows the main source of complaints was female customers between the ages of 30 and 40. It made some small changes to the packaging based on the information in the complaints. Then it decided to post a special offer for its new product on the social networking site most frequented by that target group. The chain used both competitive and customer insight to prevent product failure.

Social media offers a new way to communicate with customers. In order to stay relevant, companies must begin making changes right away.

So when trying to make a decision on where to begin, you have to experiment and get to know what possibilities exist. One way to narrow the field is to assess sites or technology against the possible benefits to you and your customers.

Question

Match each of the advantages of social media in customer-focused service to examples.

Options:

A. Deeper customer relationships

B. Immediate satisfaction
C. Competitive insights
D. Differentiated demographical experiences

Targets:

1. Customers who sign up for the loyalty program are contacted with special offers

2. The live chat offers technical help 24/7

3. The development team's newest products reflect what customers want

4. The deal offered on a site depends on the user group that most frequents it

Answer:

Using loyalty programs and special offers is an example of how using social media for customer service can help to create deeper relationships with customers.

Offering live technical help 24/7 is an example of how social media in customer service can give customers immediate satisfaction.

The new products that reflect what the customers want are an example of how a company can gain competitive insights when using customer focused social media.

A special deal offered to a specific user group and site, is an example of using social media to create a custom and group-specific experience based on the target demographic group using the site.

Measuring social media's ROI

Like any business venture, when branching out to use customer-focused social media you can expect to first make an investment. So besides assessing the benefits of social media to customer focus, you may also be able to identify ways to measure social media's return on investment, or ROI.

The costs associated with the customer-focused social media realm may include the training and hiring of employees to cover new areas of customer service. Also, there may be marketing and promotion costs, sign-up fees, and content creation costs to get your business up and running with the social media sites or technology you choose.

You may also have costs associated with the integration of new technology with existing customer service media. And to accurately track your progress, you'll also have costs connected to the analysis, monitoring, and reporting of social media success.

So to know if your investment is worth it, all these costs need to be weighed against the benefits.

Question

The bottom line for measuring the ROI of social media comes down to two main values, cost savings or revenue generating.

Do you believe this statement is true or false?

Options:

1. True
2. False

Answer:

Option 1: This option is correct. When using social media in customer service, measuring ROI can be explained in two main ideas – saving on costs or generating revenue.

Option 2: This option is incorrect. It's true that measuring ROI in social media can be expressed in two main values – costs saving or revenue generating.

The simplest way to measure the return a company receives on the investment it makes into customer-focused social media is to determine whether it's a cost savings or revenue generating move.

Once you begin to track the investment in comparison to revenue, your social media ROI will become more clear.

There are ways to track and analyze the effectiveness of social media and link it back to ROI. You can use data such as your customer retention ratio, number of issues that are identified and responded to, and your process innovations. As well, you can track the amount of content contributed, your sales, and the number of fans and followers.

Customer Focus

Tracking your customer retention ratio allows you to compare the costs of using social media to the revenue being brought in by the customers you retain through that social media channel.

You can link social media ROI directly to the number of customers you're retaining by implementing that type of social media.

For example, upgrading the company web site to offer more self service options is an expensive undertaking. However, it gives customers what they want so their retained business helps cover the costs.

Being able to track the number of issues identified and responded to helps determine if money invested into social media results in costs savings.

There's measurable ROI if the social media you use helps you answer customer questions more efficiently. Whether that's through more knowledgeable customer service representatives or other customers, the ROI is the same.

For example, creating an online company forum where customers can log issues or search past issues or FAQs to find answers more quickly. The number of issues logged and searched for can be tracked and resolution statistics evaluated.

Tracking process innovations will also help you measure social media's ROI. By monitoring company customer service processes for ways to save costs, you're able to change the processes accordingly. For example, reassigning employees as the call center gets less phone calls but the live chat function receives more interaction from customers. Finding new and innovative ways to please customers with efficient processes will help you develop a good balance of service.

Question

What are some ways to measure social media's ROI?

Options:

1. Customer retention ratio
2. Issues identified and responded to
3. Process innovations
4. Sign up fees
5. Reporting of social media success

Answer:

Option 1: This option is correct. Tracking the customer retention ratio measures the ROI of using social media to retain the revenue generated by customers.

Option 2: This option is correct. Measuring the number of issues identified and responded to will help you determine if the chosen social media is increasing efficiency which is a costs savings ROI.

Option 3: This option is correct. Analyzing and monitoring process innovations is a way to measure ROI as you balance customer service resources and save costs.

Option 4: This option is incorrect. Sign up fees are a cost to using social media for customer service.

Option 5: This option is incorrect. Reporting on the success of social media is a cost, not a way to measure ROI.

The amount of content contributed by users can also be tracked to measure social media's ROI.

If your customers are actually creating your content for free – like posting technical help solutions – that's a measurable ROI, as you would have had to pay an employee or contractor to have that content developed.

Your sales figures that are linked to a social media site should also give you some idea of a measurable ROI, like generating revenue. For example, a company uses its web site to sell promotional T-shirts associated with its best selling snack food. Online sales figures far outweigh the in-store sales. These figures reflect the ROI associated with the online store, or how well the web site is working for the company.

Finally, keeping track of the number of fans can help you measure the ROI of your social media investment. The number of followers a company or product has is a sign of how popular it is. And as fan numbers grow, so should your revenue.

But you must understand the specific rules of the social media of choice to really get a return on your investment. And you may need to offer customers an incentive to join or become a fan to initially get things started.

For example, an airline may offer free travel miles to anyone who signs up to its new web site. It may not seem to be cost effective to give valuable miles away initially until the associated revenue begins to be generated.

Tracking and monitoring these aspects of customer-focused social media helps you measure your ROI and judge the success of your social media strategy.

And having evidence that your investment paid off will allow you to continue to invest in a growing trend.

Question

What are some ways to measure social media's ROI?

Options:

1. Content contributed
2. Sales
3. Number of fans

4. Promotion

5. Employee training

Answer:

Option 1: This option is correct. Tracking the content being created by users is a way to measure ROI. Content creation is an expected cost when expanding to use social media in customer service.

Option 2: This option is correct. Tracking sales figures, especially those associated with the social media of choice, can help you measure ROI through generated revenue.

Option 3: This option is correct. The number of fans or followers your site has is one way to measure the success of your strategy and the ROI of social media.

Option 4: This option is incorrect. The amount of promotional costs is not a way to measure social media's ROI.

Option 5: This option is incorrect. Hiring and training employees is investment you should be expected to make when using social media for customer service, not a way to measure ROI.

Using knowledge management

Knowledge is often considered cognitive and intangible. And management usually involves conducting or supervising something or someone. The two concepts seem unrelated. So, how do they come together to form knowledge management, or KM?

Despite its name, knowledge management isn't really about managing other people's knowledge. It's more about gathering intellectual capital and using it to improve your business.

And, in customer-focused organizations, KM technology can help you more successfully figure out what your customers might want or need.

KM technology works by creating a system to harvest information provided by your customers. As well, it gathers information about them based on their interactions with your business. Once you use KM to gather this information, you can offer customers more, whether that's innovative products, better service, or faster answers to their questions.

There are many different types of knowledge that KM can capture:

- knowledge about the processes customers undertake and how they interact with them,
- customer preferences, what products customers are inquiring about, and what complimentary services are being provided,
- details on which products customers use and the quality of the service they receive,
- information from employees on best practices for sales and customer care, employee experiences, and the relationships they've formed, and
- internal information about employees and their skills and goals.

When considering the use of KM, you must differentiate between tacit and explicit knowledge. Tacit knowledge exists within people's minds, experience, and emotions. Explicit knowledge can be written down, recorded, archived, and protected by a company.

When implementing KM in customer interaction, all your customer information is gathered in one searchable bank of knowledge – or database – so you can quickly locate a piece of information. As well, you can add to it, to expand the knowledge contained within the bank. For example, a KM system could link issues identified during development, and after release by customers, with the solutions to the issues raised.

For customer service representatives, having a searchable bank of information enables easier and more efficient responses to customers. There's no waiting on hold and there's no need to spend extra time searching for information. Customer service representatives can simply listen and respond to the customer. This increases customer satisfaction, and decreases escalation of issues to managers and unresolved complaints.

Companies apply KM in different situations. Some companies have increased the speed with which they can solve critical operations problems by uniting remote teams through KM systems used for virtual teamwork.

Other companies have saved millions of dollars by using KM systems to share best practices with partner companies.

As well, some companies have been able to be more innovative and release products faster by harvesting ideas internally and sharing the information with development teams using KM systems.

So, there are two broad uses of KM – solving customer problems by rapidly sharing available knowledge and innovating new products and services by quickly making them commercial. As KM use grows, companies are integrating KM with customer relationship management, or CRM – a system to manage customer information to maximize profit – and having adaptive KM systems which grow and change with each new interaction. Together KM and CRM make more valuable information available for customer service.

See each use of KM to learn more.

Solving problems by sharing knowledge

Through its system of shared knowledge, KM helps solve customer problems. Tacit knowledge is made more explicit and passed on to those who could use it best. With a KM system, customer service representatives can find answers quickly and focus on bonding with customers.

Consistency in responses to customers is another benefit. No matter how a customer makes contact, the answer is the same. For example, a customer sends an e-mail and then initiates a chat and receives the same answer.

With KM, you can also create a self-service system, which uses all the knowledge the company has to "speak" to customers. More advanced KM means a more accurate response to customers' wants and needs.

Innovating new products and services

Being innovative is vital to staying competitive. If employees can gain more knowledge about their company using KM, they can figure out what can be changed. Then they may gain insight and come up with an innovative idea.

Having this knowledge also makes for a much quicker transition from idea to commercial product.

For example, KM can be used to share customer service, sales, and marketing employees' ideas with the Research and Development department.

Integrating KM with CRM

Integrating KM with CRM simply leads to happier customers. CRM and KM were once separate entities. Now, companies realize that KM is valuable to CRM and integration can result in stronger and better customer interaction.

KM's main goal is gathering knowledge to find solutions for customers; this is a natural fit for increasing the success of CRM. It's thought that over half of customer-service related costs come from the time and energy service representatives put into resolving a customer's problem or question.

If KM technologies can be integrated into the CRM system you can more easily draw from all that knowledge for a faster customer resolution. For example, a company using KM integrated with CRM found they had more first contact resolution and that customer satisfaction increased.

Having adaptive KM systems

A KM system that adapts is always "on." It's constantly capturing information and reorganizing itself, so it's actually growing and changing with each use.

Adaptive KM systems are also able to draw on a repository of knowledge to provide quick and expert answers to customers' questions. So KM offers accurate, current, and consistent responses to customers.

Choosing an adaptive KM system also comes with benefits such as an ability to be scaled to meet specific needs, flexibility, support for numerous languages, and report creation. And, an adaptive KM system should incorporate into a current CRM system easily.

Consider this example. A smartphone manufacturer decides to integrate its KM and CRM systems. An adaptive system is chosen. The main goal is first contact resolution – customers receive consistent and quick answers from a self-service system that seems like a real person. As well, a gathering tool for customer wish lists is added. Customers can request new products or services even if they don't yet exist.

Using KM systems in this way allows the company to access knowledge to solve customers' problems. This can be achieved with fast and reliable self-service without losing the personal touch.

And having the customer wish list gives the research and development team access to customers' wants and needs. This transfer of ideas and innovation can then lead to products making it to market more quickly.

Finally, integrating an adaptive KM and CRM system allows for faster customer resolution while the adaptive system blends easily with current CRM software.

So, when KM is used in customer interaction, it can solve problems, create innovation, and build knowledge.

Using KM for all these purposes will help you know your customers better. And then you'll be able to give them what they need, possibly even before they know they need it.

Question

Which statements describe the uses of knowledge management in customer interaction?

Options:

1. Products and services get to market more quickly due to innovation based on knowledge
2. Access to information is immediate, making customer problem solving more rapid
3. CRM integration makes customer data available to customer service
4. Systems adapt to customer information and data
5. Inventory is tracked and monitored nationwide
6. Loyal customers are rewarded with special offers

Answer:

Option 1: This option is correct. You can use the knowledge gained through KM to come up with innovative ideas that can transition to commercial products quickly.

Option 2: This option is correct. You can solve customer problems more quickly when using KM to gather information in one searchable bank.

Option 3: This option is correct. Integrating KM and CRM gathers customer information together, giving you even better insight into what your customers want.

Option 4: This option is correct. Using adaptive KM systems brings your technology to another level as information is gathered and the KM system is constantly growing and changing.

Option 5: This option is incorrect. KM systems are not used to track inventory but can be used to monitor sales and customer comments on products.

Option 6: This option is incorrect. Presenting deals or offers to loyal customers is a benefit of using social media in customer interactions.

Benefits of knowledge management

With knowledge management, once you understand the use, it's important to explore the different KM technologies and software tools. Then you can create a strategy for how KM can be perfected for your purposes in customer interaction. And once your KM system is in place, you'll begin to recognize the benefits of using KM in a customer-focused environment.

Since KM is used to solve problems, create innovation, and build knowledge, it only stands to reason that the main benefits stem from these uses. Using a KM system helps your company provide efficient and consistent customer service interactions. As well, you can use KM to retain existing customers and win new ones. Finally, KM helps improve processes by making valuable information available to those executing the process.

See the benefits of using KM in a customer-focused environment for more information.

Provide efficient and consistent interactions

When using KM, and especially adaptive KM, a company can create a truly customer-focused system. Customers get the answers they're seeking quickly, easily, and reliably, the first time.

The bank of information customers have to draw from allows customer service representatives to be more efficient. They're also able to give consistent responses over many types of interaction channels – such as chat, e-mail, phone, or self-service.

Retain and win customers

KM can increase the number of customers who have a positive resolution experience the first time. Those customers will not only remain loyal but may also recommend the company to friends. Customers often reach out through social media to spread positive comments.

Improve processes

A benefit of using KM that goes hand-in-hand with positive interactions and retaining customers is improved processes. A successful KM system makes valuable information available to those executing the process, thereby increasing the process's efficiency.

Customer service representatives, interacting with customers via phone, e-mail, forums, blogs, or live chats, are able to quickly and expertly access valuable information. This allows them to spend less time searching and more time connecting with customers. It also cuts down on employee frustration and irate customers waiting on hold for long periods of time.

Consider this example. A fitness center chain has a web site where members can log in and see schedules and upcoming events, pay their fees, and send e-mail queries.

As the company grows, members begin to want more. And the fitness trainers, who function as the main contacts for customer service, want access to more information. The chain decides to upgrade the web site and integrate KM technology with the existing CRM system.

The new web site, using KM technology with CRM, is launched with additional functions for members to track their progress, search for new fitness programs, and chat with other members or trainers.

And the adaptive KM system provides members with a convenient searchable bank full of valuable knowledge. As well, when members log in to the site, they receive notifications tailored to their favorite gym activities and fitness levels.

The trainers find the upgrade beneficial too. They like being able to access so much member information in one place and find they spend more time connecting with members. They especially notice an increase in new members due to positive recommendations from current members.

The bank of knowledge made for more efficient and consistent interactions between trainers and members.

As well, the new web site improved processes for both members and trainers. Members could complete more tasks and everyone could access more information that was useful to them. Also, the adaptive system grew from the gathered knowledge and could provide members with information tailored to their profiles.

Finally, the positive member interactions, both online and with trainers, led to recommendations from members, which resulted in new applicants. So the KM system

Customer Focus

helped the fitness chain retain existing customers and win new ones.

Question

What are examples of the benefits of KM in a customer-focused service?

Options:

1. Customer service representatives complete more first-time resolutions

2. Members leave positive comments on a blog which leads to an increase in new clients

3. Customers find solutions to technical issues quickly in a bank of logged issues

4. Customers receive technical help by phone and different information via live chat

5. Human resources employees search separate departmental databases to view HR files

Answer:

Option 1: This option is correct. A benefit to using KM systems is that customer service representatives are able to solve customer issues more efficiently and consistently.

Option 2: This option is correct. Retaining customers and an increased number of new customers is a benefit of using KM.

Option 3: This option is correct. Improved processes, such as searching for technical help, is a benefit to using KM.

Option 4: This option is incorrect. With KM, customers should not receive different information via different channels of communication. A benefit of KM is information being passed along efficiently and consistently.

Option 5: This option is incorrect. A benefit of using KM is gathering information in a single bank to increase efficiency and consistency. Searching separate databases is not a benefit of using KM.

Mobile technology in customer service

Most people have a variety of mobile devices that are vital to their daily lives. Customers expect to be able to access support any time they need. Mobile devices are yet another way that companies can connect with customers and provide them better service on the customer's terms.

Consider this example. A camera manufacturer notices more customers making contact through their smartphones. So it decides to adapt its customer service accordingly. First, it adapts its web site technology for easier access with a mobile device. This way all customers, even those using smartphones with smaller screens, can access the same information. As well, it created a self-service system available 24/7. Finally, the company integrated its systems to give customers access to a repository of technical help and tips.

Knowing how to provide content more easily to customers is one advantage to understanding how to apply mobile technology to customer service. The camera manufacturer changed the technology so more customers could access the same support content. It took into account how customers were reaching out, and changed the customer service options to suit them.

Understanding how to give 24/7 access to customers is another advantage to understanding the connection between mobile technology and customer service. Both customers and service and support employees of the camera manufacturer were able to access the required information anytime and anywhere. As well, by creating a self-service system that was easy for customers to use, it didn't have to have hours of operation, but could truly be 24/7.

Finally, by recognizing how the technology could be used to build customer rapport, the camera manufacturer discovered another advantage to linking mobile technology to customer service. Offering easy access to an effective knowledge repository created a large group of happy customers. This type of customer service can retain customers and bring you new ones.

Question

What are the advantages of understanding how mobile technology is applied in customer service?

Options:

1. You know how to provide content more easily to customers

2. You understand how to give access to customers 24/7

3. You recognize how the technology can be used to build rapport

4. You know more customers' second point of contact

5. You realize how many different types of technological systems are available

Answer:

Option 1: This option is correct. It's advantageous to you to understand how to use mobile technology in customer service so you're able to provide a broader spectrum of service content to your customers.

Option 2: This option is correct. You'll be at an advantage if you can understand how best to offer customers access to service and support, 24/7, through mobile technology.

Option 3: This option is correct. Understanding how you can use mobile technology to build rapport, by satisfying your customers with faster, more accurate responses, is an advantage in customer service.

Option 4: This option is incorrect. Having customer information, like a second point of contact phone number, is not an advantage to understanding how mobile technology is applied in customer service.

Option 5: This option is incorrect. Realizing there are many types of technological systems to choose from is not an advantage to understanding how mobile technology is applied in customer service.

Key concepts of mobile CRM

Although not every mobile user has the most up-to-date device, all users have at least the basic capabilities of mobile technology. Smartphones are now used as your computer, phone, e-mail, TV, and newspaper. Indeed, people now spend more time connected via their mobile devices than online. Customer relationship management, or CRM, needs to adapt to this trend.

Mobile technologies are able to provide instant customer service. By integrating mobile technology into your CRM systems, your business can increase its responsiveness to customers.

For example, a service technician on the road can respond to help customers with small problems, suggest fixes, schedule service calls, and even reset some problems internally through his mobile device.

Also, customers can download self-service programs and applications to their mobile devices. So then customers can make enquiries even while away from their computers. For example, a customer away on business, waiting in an airport, can change his cable TV packages via the self-service options through his mobile device.

And the newest trend is geolocation. This technology works with GPS-enabled smartphones to allow the user to check in to locations such as businesses, restaurants, or museums. Customers can then make comments and view suggestions of other places they might like, based on where they are.

Mobile CRM can bring a number of advantages to business. A few key concepts to consider are that mobile devices help build CRM databases. Also, customer opt-in leads to deeper CRM system penetration. In addition, the personal nature of mobile technology increases mobile CRM value.

See each key concept involved in mobile CRM for more information.

Mobile devices build CRM databases

Customer information received through mobile devices can add to CRM databases. A part of KM and CRM integration is the constant addition of information to the searchable repository.

When you develop mobile CRM, you can use every mobile device as one more point of contact with your customers. So, for every query made via a mobile device, customers provide data which gets added to the CRM bank.

Customer opt-in leads to CRM penetration

Many mobile providers require customers to choose to opt-in when subscribing, or to give their permission to receive offers and advertisements via their mobile devices. This additional point of contact allows for deeper CRM system penetration. In other words, more information can be passed back and forth to your customers.

This new channel for customers to receive messages, offers, deals, and ads can quickly add up in sales figures or brand recognition.

Personal technology increases CRM value

Many mobile device users regard their phone as a much more personal device than, for example, their e-mail or their television. That's why the one-to-one personal nature of mobile technology increases its value.

Receiving a message through a mobile device taps into that personal nature of the technology. People are less likely to immediately dismiss a message via their mobile device. This enables mobile CRM to make a personal connection with the customer.

Consider this example. A home decor and furniture store creates an application for customers to view weekly ads, make shopping lists, and check if items are in stock. Every time a customer uses the application, the CRM system receives more information about the customer. The store can send those customers special offers via their mobile devices for increased sales and branding. Mobile CRM enables the company to learn something new about customers every time they use the application on their mobile devices.

This particular application for smartphone customers of the home decor and furniture store helped add information to the CRM database. Each time customers log in, the information they access is recorded in the system as well as any searches, changes, or queries they make. And this information can then, in turn, be used by the store for marketing, promotion, or buying.

Customer Focus

A part of downloading the application and creating a profile involves agreeing to receive information from the store. This opt-in offers the store another way to access their customers. Through this communication path the store can not only send information but can also receive more details about customers.

Finally, the personal nature of the application adds CRM value. Each time a customer logs in and accesses their personal profile, they might get a special offer via text message for an item they're interested in, or perhaps a reminder that appears on their smartphone for a specific sale that's about to end, thereby enhancing the personal connection.

Question

What are some of the key positive developments associated with mobile CRM?

Options:

1. Mobile devices provide information to build CRM databases
2. Customers opt-in for deeper penetration
3. Value is increased due to the personal nature of the technology
4. Customers spend more time connected via mobile devices
5. Mobile devices are used in sales and field service

Answer:

Option 1: This option is correct. A key concept of mobile CRM in customer service is that every contact customers make through a mobile device adds to the CRM repository.

Option 2: This option is correct. When customers subscribe to mobile packages, they often opt-in to receive additional ads or messages which allow for deeper penetration of mobile CRM systems.

Option 3: This option is correct. Customers often feel their mobile device is much more personal than their e-mail or TV. Messages received via mobile CRM are viewed more often than dismissed. And this increases mobile CRM value.

Option 4: This option is incorrect. It's correct that often customers spend more time connected through mobile devices than online, but this isn't a key concept of mobile CRM.

Option 5: This option is incorrect. Traditionally mobile CRM was used in sales and field service, but that's not a key concept of mobile CRM.

Mobile access to primary business solutions, including CRM, is an imperative in today's hugely competitive business world. Traditionally, mobile CRM has been used in two areas, sales and field service. However, it could expand across other areas. Businesses need to consider not only what mobile CRM can currently do, but how it may help address customers' needs in the future.

Consider some of the ways mobile CRM has developed. For example, it can be used for account and contact management. You could use your mobile device to view accounts and contacts, add new contacts, and make comments on account activity.

Also, mobile CRM in integrated calendar management can schedule activities and tag them when completed.

And mobile CRM in customer service ticket management enables customers to receive a ticket on logging a request for support. Then they can view open support tickets and track issues as they are closed upon resolution.

When considering using mobile technology in customer service and integrating mobile CRM, it's important to also consider some of the risks involved. Using mobile CRM requires a careful examination of your business's core strategy to ensure its use aligns with your business's current and future direction.

See each concern about mobile CRM to learn more about it.

Rapid change brings instability with innovation

Mobile CRM, like most technological advances, is changing quickly, and this rapid innovation creates a certain amount of instability.

New products and software are being released and reworked all the time with better options or more flexibility.

The technology you choose should be considered ahead of time to ensure it's the best choice for your business at the time of implementation.

Mobile CRM requires an examination of strategy

When exploiting the potential of mobile CRM you need to carry out a careful examination of your business's core strategy.

You should determine the end goals and strategy of your business in the short and long term. This will give you a better view of how you should integrate mobile CRM into your customer service strategy.

This examination will help you get the most out of the mobile CRM technology you choose and your investment.

For example, a corporate bank wants to implement mobile CRM technology so businesses can manage expense accounts more easily via mobile devices. A team of executives discover three different types of software that might suit the bank's needs. They also examine the bank's core business strategy – to provide innovative business solutions to its customers.

Of the three types of software being reviewed, the first is on budget but lacks some of the newer innovation. The second is a new release, adaptable, and highly expensive from an award winning company. And the third is also a new release, virtually unknown, but on budget.

The bank executives are concerned about the instability of the industry. They wonder if it makes sense to wait another six months. By then the technology may have again grown and changed and software that's a better fit might be available.

As well, they examine the potential costs savings to try to decide if they're too great to pass up – in other words, if investing now in a higher priced but innovative product would save in the long run.

The bank's core strategy is to provide innovative business solutions to its customers. This means allowing its customers to manage employee expense accounts, approve limit raises, and receive alerts on overspending.

Once the bank's executives start to focus on the end goals, they can more easily wade through the software available to choose exactly what's suited to them.

After meeting a few more times, they weighed the costs versus returns and the risks involved with choosing among competing technologies. As well, by determining the bank's strategy in implementing mobile CRM, they were able to avoid being limited by the technology. They addressed their business goals first and foremost. They chose an expensive but powerful CRM technology that could be adapted to future applications in order to get the most out of their investment.

Question

What are some of the key concerns associated with mobile CRM?

Options:

1. Rapid industry change brings instability with innovation

2. An examination of a business's core strategy is required before exploiting the potential of mobile CRM

3. Advanced innovation requires a larger investment

4. Lack of mobile CRM increases customer dissatisfaction

Answer:

Option 1: This option is correct. The mobile CRM and technological industry is changing and advanced innovation is appearing rapidly. Because of this, the industry can be unstable, so businesses must take that change and instability into account when considering mobile CRM integration.

Option 2: This option is correct. If a business first examines the core strategy and current and end goals, it'll be better able to choose the correct mobile CRM technology.

Option 3: This option is incorrect. It's not always correct that advanced innovation will require a larger investment but this idea is not a key concept associated with mobile CRM.

Option 4: This option is incorrect. Whether or not choosing not to integrate CRM technology increases customer dissatisfaction is not a key concept associated with mobile CRM.

GLOSSARY

Glossary
C
CEO - See chief executive officer.

change management process - A sequence of steps or activities that a change management team or project leader follows to apply change management to a project.

chief executive officer - The highest ranking executive or corporate officer within an organization who is in charge of total management of the company. Typically, the chief executive officer reports to the organization's board of directors.

CRM - See customer relationship management.

customer - The recipient of a product, a service, or information supplied by the seller or selling organization.

customer focus - A commitment to improve products or services on an ongoing basis, based on customer needs and requirements.

customer relationship management - The knowledge an organization possesses about its customers' requirements and expectations, and how this knowledge is used to maximize customer satisfaction and improve processes and strategies, to maximize profit.

customer satisfaction survey - The process of discovering whether or not an organization's customers are happy or satisfied with the products or services received from the company. May be conducted face to face, over the phone, via e-mail or Internet, or on handwritten forms. Customer answers to questions are then used to analyze whether or not changes need to be made in business operations to increase overall satisfaction.

E

explicit knowledge - Any information that can be written down, recorded, archived, and protected by a company.

F

focus group - A qualitative research method where current or potential customers are invited to participate in a structured discussion, led by a trained facilitator. Usually a group of six to twelve participants.

G

geolocation - Mobile technology that works with GPS-enabled smartphones to locate users through their phone. Geolocation can also be enabled using cell tower triangulation when GPS is unavailable. Applications allow a user to check in to locations and make comments or receive suggestions from friends on other places of interest based on where the user is.

K

KM - See knowledge management.

knowledge management - A framework for designing an organization's strategy, structures, and processes so that the organization can use what it knows to learn and to create value for its customers. See KM.

L

lost-account surveys - The process of discovering why former customers decide not to do business with an organization anymore through individual interviews. Interviews are conducted by telephone or in person, rather than e-mail, and aim to discover specific reasons why customers were displeased with the organization.

R

return on investment - Return on investment, or ROI, is a measure for determining how successful an initiative is, compared to how much you have spent. ROI is calculated by determining the amount invested in a project or initiative relative to the benefits it generates. Social media ROI measures the amount of benefit social media customer service efforts return to an organization. See ROI.

ROI - See return on investment.

S

Six Sigma - An operational strategy for organizations that focuses on minimizing variability in manufacturing and business processes, such as customer service. The aim is to make these processes error-free.

W

web site UI - See web site user interface.

web site user interface - The visual element of a web site through which a user interacts with the web site, covering all commands and icons.

REFERENCES

References
Customer Care Excellence: How to Create an Effective Customer Focus, 5th Edition - 2008, Sarah Cook, Kogan
The Outside-In Corporation: How to Build a Customer-Centric Organization for Breakthrough Results - 2006, Barbara E. Bund, McGraw-Hill
CRM at the Speed of Light: Social CRM Strategies, Tools, and Techniques for Engaging Your Customers, Fourth Edition - 2010 , Paul Greenberg, McGraw-Hill/Osborne
Designing the Customer-Centric Organization: A Guide to Strategy, Structure, and Process - 2005, Jay Galbraith, Jossey-Bass
CRM: Customer Relationship Mobile - http://www.destinationcrm.com/Articles/Web-Exclusives/Viewpoints/CRM-Customer-Relationship-Mobile---60572.aspx

Customer Focus

Knowledge Management: making sense of an oxymoron
http://www.skyrme.com/insights/22km.htm

www.ingramcontent.com/pod-product-compliance
Lightning Source LLC
Chambersburg PA
CBHW020914180526
45163CB00007B/2733